Finding Identity Through Directing

Finding Identity Through Directing is a practice-led autoethnographical monograph that provides an in-depth exploration into the field of theatre directing and an individual's endless creative pursuit for belonging. The book specifically examines how a culturally displaced individual may find a sense of identity through directing and addresses the internal struggles of belonging, acceptance and Self that are often experienced by those who have confronted cultural unhoming. The first half of the book scrutinises Dr Yekanians' own identity as an Iranian-born Armenian-Australian and how she struggled with belonging growing up in a world that, for the most part, was unaccepting of her differences. The second half looks at how theatre directing aided her (re)discovery of Self. While evidence shows that within the past decade there has been a growing interest in the vocation of theatre directing, embarking on a career within this field, while exciting, can often be a daunting and experimental vocation. *Finding Identity Through Directing* questions this conundrum and specifically asks, in a competitive artistic profession that is rapidly developing, what attracts an individual to the authoritative role of the director and what are the underlying motivations of this attraction? By uncovering that there is more to the role of the director than the mere finality of a production, we can observe that the theatre is a promising setting for cultural exchanges in dialogue and for personal development. Theatre directing as the vehicle for these expansions and progressions of self can potentially address the internal struggles of identity often experienced by those who, in some form, have encountered cultural displacement.

Dr Soseh Yekanians is a theatre director and academic whose research focuses on understandings of Self, belonging and identity formation with specific reference to theatre directing. She is also fascinated with how theatre and the performing arts more generally can speak to an individual's sense of displacement. Dr Yekanians hopes that with more research on how cultural stereotypes manifest in individuals through the pressures of society and how these stereotypes are performed via theatrical representations onstage, performance as a cultural phenomenon can begin to break down harmful stereotypes and offer cross-cultural exchanges that develop and empower people's (re)discovery of identity offstage.

Finding Identity Through Directing

Soseh Yekanians

LONDON AND NEW YORK

First published 2020
by Routledge
2 Park Square, Milton Park, Abingdon, Oxon OX14 4RN

and by Routledge
52 Vanderbilt Avenue, New York, NY 10017

Routledge is an imprint of the Taylor & Francis Group, an informa business

© 2020 Soseh Yekanians

The right of Soseh Yekanians to be identified as author of this work has been asserted by her in accordance with sections 77 and 78 of the Copyright, Designs and Patents Act 1988.

All rights reserved. No part of this book may be reprinted or reproduced or utilised in any form or by any electronic, mechanical, or other means, now known or hereafter invented, including photocopying and recording, or in any information storage or retrieval system, without permission in writing from the publishers.

Trademark notice: Product or corporate names may be trademarks or registered trademarks, and are used only for identification and explanation without intent to infringe.

British Library Cataloguing-in-Publication Data
A catalogue record for this book is available from the British Library

Library of Congress Cataloging-in-Publication Data
Names: Yekanians, Soseh, author.
Title: Finding identity through directing / Soseh Yekanians.
Description: Abingdon, Oxon ; New York, NY : Routledge, 2020. | Includes bibliographical references.
Identifiers: LCCN 2019059982
Subjects: LCSH: Yekanians, Soseh. | Theatrical producers and directors—Psychology. | Theater—Production and direction—Psychological aspects. | Identity (Psychology) | Belonging (Social psychology)
Classification: LCC PN2053 .Y48 2020 | DDC 792.02/33092 [B]—dc23
LC record available at https://lccn.loc.gov/2019059982

ISBN: 978-0-367-17315-9 (hbk)
ISBN: 978-0-429-05615-4 (ebk)

Typeset in Times New Roman
by Apex CoVantage, LLC

To my *extra*-ordinary parents, I will never be able to repay you for the sacrifices you made and continue to make for me – for coming to this great country [Australia] in the first place and giving up your ambitions so that I could follow mine. If only every parent were that selfless. Սիրտիս տակից մէրսի ամէն ինչից, այս գրածքը ձեր անունով է:

Not all those who wander are lost.

– J. R. R. Tolkien (1954)

Contents

List of figures ix
Foreword by Lyndall Adams x
Preface xiii
Acknowledgements xiv

Introduction 1

Field of study 1
Structure of the book 4
Methodology 5
    Practice-led research 6
    Tacit knowledge 7
    Autoethnography and reflexivity 8
    The interviews 9
    In summary 11
References 11

1 Attracted to theatre: setting the scene 13

Prologue 13
The essence of theatre 14
Theatre as a social construct 17
The theatre and me 19
References 22

2 Seeking identity: searching for self 24

Identifying identity 24
What's in a home? 30
Belonging and displacement 33
Flirting with the "unhomely" and the "in-between" 35

viii   *Contents*

   The other 37
   References 41

3 **Affinity with Armenia: a narrative in two parts**   44

   Part I: what went before 44
      Birth of a nation 44
      The beginnings of the invaders 46
      The Armenian Genocide 47
      The Republic of Armenia today 51
   My voyage from a dream to reality 52
      September 2008 52
   Part II: the journey back 54
      September 2014 54
      A New Armenia or a new me? 55
   References 61

4 **Dating directing: finding the perfect match**   64

   Deconstructing directing 64
      Background 64
      Collaborative research through the Kitchen Sink Collective 68
      Turning points in the research 70
         Moment one 70
         Moment two 72
   To be or not to be 73
      Homing versus belonging 75
      The director's journey 79
   Immersion into the practice of directing 81
      No Worries and *Uncle Jack* 81
         Background 81
         Stereotype, defamiliarisation and difference 83
   References 93

   Conclusion   95

   Final thoughts 100

   Appendix 102

   Interview questions from phase 1 102
   Interview questions from phase 2 103
   Full list of theatre directors interviewed 104

   Index   105

Figures

3.1	Laora's kitchen, pantry, spare room and front yard in Tsaghkadzor (2014)	58
4.1	My portrayal of the "director's spiral of creation within the theatre"	78
4.2	Georgia Metternick-Jones (2013), set (from *No Worries*)	86
4.3	Hannah Metternick-Jones (2013), costume sketches (from *No Worries*)	86
4.4	Production still (2014) (from *Uncle Jack*)	87
4.5	Production still (2014) (from *Uncle Jack*)	88
4.6	Production still (2013) (from *No Worries*)	90

Foreword

I am a fairly poor correspondent. Not through indifference. Being time poor is also a feeble excuse. Social media keeps me connected . . . enough. Then again, some conversations are unbroken. When I met this scholar in the making, I had an overload of postgraduate students. I wondered how I would ever manage. This one got under my skin. All shiny eyes and hair. Red lips and a smile so big that her nose crinkles. Soseh Yekanians is an actor and director with a voice trained to be heard. A personality big enough to fill a room. A Persian-Armenian-Australian at times wedged in between cultures.

What could bring us together in such close connection? Four-ish years on a PhD, yes. But I am a contemporary visual artist and academic, specialising in practice-led research. A phenomenologist interested in working with the body, the female body, the lived body that is determined and specific. My arts practice speaks to the lively concerns of feminisms, the day-to-day running of the lived body in a state of flux, defined and redefined by changing practices and discourses. In the studio, I rehearse the world through the body, performing the senses (sight, touch and memory) and making them visible and tangible (Meskimmon, 2003). Yekanians rehearses the world through the theatre. The discourses with which I work implicate contemporary arts practice in situated narratives than picture the ways I walk around in the world. Very much akin to the worlds Yekanians builds. As Terry Smith says,

> In contemporaneity, world-picturing, place-making, and connectivity take many forms, tend in many directions. And operate in many dimensions, but keep circulating back to the four main themes that preoccupy contemporary artists: the changing sense of what it is to be in time, to be located or on the move, to find freedom within mediation, to piece together a sense of self from the fragmented strangeness that is all around us.
>
> (2009, p. 235)

What is this book? A book about self-discovery and bringing the pieces of that fragmented strangeness into communication. A book about directing. A book about the process of cultural loss and recovery inside and outside the theatre. A book about dislocation. A book about Armenia. But mostly, it is a book about courage, resilience and passion. An eloquent exploration of the Armenian Genocide and its centrality to Armenian cultural identity, which raises questions about the politics of memory and belonging. A life made through the rubbled ruins of a place lost to the author. And yet it is a heritage that does not take no for an answer. No one else could write this book. An academic text, yes. But. An insight into the world of the diasporic. A herstory of the Armenian dispersion.

Watching Yekanians's trepidation as she prepared for her return to Armenia in 2014 gave me pause to reflect on just how significant this research was. Notions around *displacement*, the *other*, *belonging*, the *unhomely* and the *in-between* inform this narrative – themes that many individuals experience – enabling the reflexive praxis required to undertake such a brave journey of self-discovery. In this case an uneasy and at times painful Armenian self, which was extended through interviews with directors from multicultural backgrounds. These interviews are a fascinating insight into finding identity through the theatre and more than a glimpse at understanding the role of the director.

Dr Joyce Van Dyke from Harvard University examined the original PhD thesis. Van Dyke was unfamiliar with the academic *autoethnographical* approach taken but was persuaded of its validity and importance in its attempt to draw a circle around a fluid and indeterminate complex of ideas and experiences and to do justice to the not always mappable stages of the creative process. This thesis, in her view, was an ambitious, searching, honest and courageous project. In investigating the nexus of creative/artistic endeavour and personal development, especially in the *hidden* field of theatre directing, Yekanians expands the traditional purview of scholarly research and investigation. In particular, her questions about the motivation to become a theatre director in relation to one's own cultural displacement are, to Van Dyke's knowledge, both original and illuminating.

The methodology may seem to be simply an academic mechanism. It is, in many ways. What may not be readily apparent to many readers is the paucity of methodological writing in this field. Some may skip over this part, while some struggling to find their way through such a complex process will find it invaluable whether they reside inside or outside the theatre. The multi-method approach tailored to directorial practice is outlined in the introduction. This narrative scaffolds our understanding of the whole. It is woven together through the loom of interviews (Phases 1 and 2), the trip to Armenia (Phase 3), practice and literature reviews, journaling, the practice of directing, archival research for the director and creative development.

Van Dyke found the whole topic of theatre practice as a solvent for cultural displacement for all theatre practitioners, not just directors, something she would like to read and think more about. As for me, the narrating of Yekanians' personal journey, both literal and metaphorical, into her Armenian self makes for moving and provocative reading. The story told is honest, intimate and powerful.

Lyndall Adams, PhD
Director, CREAtec (Centre for Research in Entertainment,
Arts, Technology, Education and Communication)
Senior Research Fellow
School of Arts and Humanities and Western Australian
Academy of Performing Arts
Edith Cowan University
Perth, Australia

References

Meskimmon, M. (2003). *Women making art: history, subjectivity, aesthetics.* London; New York: Routledge.
Smith, T. (2009). *What is Contemporary Art?* Chicago: The University of Chicago Press.

Preface

It is suggested that artistic research is often motivated by emotional, personal and subjective concerns, operating not only on the basis of explicit and exact knowledge but also on that of tacit knowledge (Barrett & Bolt, 2010). Therefore, while I understand that there may be many motivations for becoming a director, *Finding Identity Through Directing* ultimately rediscovers what my role and purpose as a theatre director in Australia were and how the impetus to choose this profession (or how it chose me) may have been linked to my struggles as a culturally displaced Persian-Armenian-Australian growing up in a world that, at the time, I felt was not accepting of my differences. The research, however, also partly redresses the paucity of scholarly material available in the area of theatre directing and addresses cultural effects relating to individuals who have struggled with ethnic identity and displacement by offering innovative insight into the possible motivations of theatre directors. This knowledge can increase emerging directors' understanding of the complexity of their craft and perhaps lead them to question consciously their own provocations. If the motivation is triggered by a search for identity, then how might this propulsion inform the plays they choose and their artistic vision and influence the methods they employ in the rehearsal room to achieve that level of expression?

In due course, by uncovering that there is more to the role of the director than the mere finality of a production, we can observe that the theatre is a promising setting for cultural exchanges in dialogue and for personal development. Theatre directing as the vehicle for these expansions and progressions of self can potentially address the internal struggles of identity often experienced by those who, in some form, have encountered cultural displacement. In doing so, we may have the opportunity to utilise the theatre as a space for communal exchanges and conversations where we can begin to open up a dialogue that initiates difference.

My hopes are that this book will help individuals who have been a product of migration or those who have simply faced similar daily struggles of self-criticism due to bullying and discrimination inflicted by others appreciate that their differences should be a source of celebration, not shame, and, more importantly, through the theatre this endless (re)discovery is possible.

Reference

Barrett, E. & Bolt, B. (2010). *Practice as research: Approaches to creative arts enquiry.* New York, NY: Tauris.

Acknowledgements

Firstly, I would like to thank Associate Professor Andrew Lewis at the Western Australian Academy of Performing Arts (WAAPA) in Perth who, in 2012, created an opportunity for me to be able to embark on a life-changing journey as a director-researcher. From our initial meeting at the Sydney auditions to the four years I spent at WAAPA, you were always a great supporter of my work, and for that, I thank you.

Secondly, to my formidable principal supervisors, Associate Professor Maggi Phillips and Dr Lyndall Adams, both of whom were incredible mentors, guides and friends during my PhD. Sadly, Maggi passed away in March 2015 just before I completed the first draft of my thesis; however, her selfless wisdom, guidance and belief stayed with me well beyond our conversations in which she would often say, "Life is not just black and white, Soseh; you need to see the grey in everything". These exchanges taught me that life is full of endless possibilities and that, as a researcher, I should never stop being curious. This is a lesson that I will forever carry with me. Your cynical voice and hearty laugh are never too far from my thoughts, Maggi.

Lyndall, my goodness, where do I start? You were written on my forehead and I on yours. You were my supervisor, my colleague, my surrogate mother, my friend, my therapist, my teammate, my cheerleader, my voice of reason, the balloon to my sandbags and my rock. There were so many moments in this journey when I was full of doubt, but you *never* lost faith in my abilities – not even once.

Thirdly, to the directors who allowed me to pry into their lives and shared their perspectives on the profession, thank you for your invaluable contributions towards this study. Similarly, to the countless actors who were a part of the various creative projects that occurred during this period, I thank you for your trust and enthusiasm.

And, finally, to all my other friends, family and supporters who were on this incomparable journey, thanks for sharing in the laughter, fears and dreams, but most of all for keeping me *transparent*.

Introduction

Field of study

Although the timing and rise of the director's role in theatre is uncertain, throughout history, there are abundant illustrations of how the director's presence within the theatre has taken form (T. Cole & Chinoy, 1953). As elusive as the director's historic position within the milieu of theatre appears to be, within the past few decades, there has been a growing interest in theatre directing. This is in part due to an increasing number of institutions offering courses in directing. The combination of these courses, the push for entrepreneurial enterprise by the global creative industries and a growing individual curiosity into the role of the director has encouraged growth within this creative art form. However, although there is growing documentation into the role of the director, for the most part, it has remained an almost hidden profession (Cole, 1992). In such a creative climate, this book explores the possible underlying motivations into why individuals pursue a path into this profession and the probable connection between theatre directing and an individual's personal pursuit of identity. The title of this book, *Finding Identity Through Directing*, points to how directing as an authoritative profession can provide a sense of identity and belonging that addresses the internal struggles individuals encounter through cultural displacement, and if perchance theatre directing does offer such individuals an avenue for self-exploration, then how does the experience(s) facilitate them in reconciling themselves to the world in which they are situated?

My directing story began when I came to Australia at 18 months old. Supposedly, arriving at such a tender age gave me plenty of time to forget my Armenian background and integrate completely into the Australian culture. However, I was raised in an Armenian household where I was not only taught to read, write and speak the Armenian language but also raised within all its traditions. Deserting my Armenian heritage was not a possibility. Indeed, in conjunction with *normal* school, I attended Saturday school for nine years to learn more about my Armenian culture: its histories, philosophies, etymology and dialect. Additionally, I did not look like my perception of the stereotypical Australian, with my dark eyes and dark hair. Moving through childhood into adolescence and then adulthood, I began to feel more and more out of place. I was a Christian Armenian born in the Islamic

Republic of Iran and raised in democratic Australia. I did not identify with any of these cultures and, instead, felt stuck between them. Being somehow connected to all yet truly belonging to none. Throughout this book, I discuss these matters further as their relevance emerges as key aspects of the research. Not only did these concerns affect my sense of identity, but they also affected my work as an actor and theatre director. Furthermore, what I did not recognise at the time was that while I felt "Australia" was positioning me as an outsider within its community, I was positioning myself as an outsider within my Armenian community, hence segregating myself from both cultures. In the theatre, however, none of my cultural reservations or my anxieties seemed to matter. In fact, being "the other" became somewhat interesting, and my personal story of the Armenian whose family left Iran after the Islamic Revolution suddenly gained traction and, at times, was an outright advantage. The social stigmas attached to the *other* rapidly began to fade, and through theatre, I reinvented myself.

In the present day, to say that I have decisively found a sense of belonging and complete sense of self would be erroneous, as I continue to struggle with a sense of cultural displacement. Within the theatre, however, and through my work as a theatre director, these struggles have become less prominent. Although I have not found a definitive answer regarding my sense of dislocation, through the theatre, I have been able to find a sense of contentment. Yet embarking on a profession in the theatre and in theatre directing, while exciting, can often be a daunting and experimental vocation. Polish Australian actor and director Bogdan Koca once acknowledged that the loneliness of theatre was something that he thought about a great deal:

> There is no life outside what we are doing here.... That is the madness, the stupidity of theatre.... It's a collective work, but it's the most lonely profession that exists.... You don't know where the border is between performance and life.
>
> (as cited in Evans, 1987, p. 2)

Similarly, in reference to directing, renowned Australian director Gale Edwards said, "Being a director can be a very hard job: it's lonely, it's isolated, you are responsible if anything goes wrong, you are forgotten when everything goes right, you're attacked by critics" (as cited in Ward, 1988, p. 11). Both Koca and Edwards noted the isolation and immense responsibilities associated with the vocation. However, I do not completely agree with their statements, for although there is considerable loneliness and accountability within the theatre and in the role of the director, there is also solace, joy, companionship and pleasure in working with a collective. Nevertheless, both Koca's and Edwards's remarks and the growing interest in the field of directing over the past decade compelled me to question the vocation of theatre directing in-depth and to probe into the underlying motivations that draw an individual into the creative field.

In addition, beyond the direct association with theatre directing, this research has great significance for me as an Armenian. This autoethnographical study began with my narrative as an Armenian-Australian and propelled me on a journey of (re) discovery of my ethnic identity. What I had not anticipated was that the original thesis would near completion at an historic moment. The 100th anniversary of the Armenian Genocide occurred on 24 April 2015, and the discussions that led up to that occasion were internationally broadcast. For the first time in many years, widespread deliberations on the 1915 massacres were taking place because Armenia was being represented in the European Court of Human Rights to fight the denial of the Armenian Genocide by Turks (Squires, 2015). Further, these discussions surrounding Armenia and diasporic Armenians were moving beyond politics and becoming widespread conversations through various artistic projects. On 14 April 2015, photojournalist Scout Tufankjian (2015) published a book called *There Is Only the Earth: Images from the Armenian Diaspora Project* about her four years of travel documenting Armenian communities in such countries as the United States, Lebanon, Armenia, Ethiopia and Brazil, aiming to tell the story of the Armenian people.

Tufankjian notes that displacement and upheaval are not new challenges for Armenians, as they date to 3,000 years ago when Armenians left their ancestral homes in Eastern Turkey and Northern Syria to follow ancient trade and pilgrimage routes while also fleeing countless revolutions, civil wars and massacres (2014). Yet with all this, she affirms that today's Armenian diaspora is strong and vibrant with over eight million Armenians living all over the globe. "As a child, it was inexplicable to me why none of the literature on Armenians reflected this complexity. Instead, it was all just about the massacres – as if the Genocide had successfully ended the Armenian story" (Tufankjian, 2014, Mission section, para. 1). For Tufankjian, it was vital that although the Armenians had been largely known only for their role as the victims in one of the first genocides of the twentieth century, her project was not about victimhood; it was a portrait of survival (2014).

Like Tufankjian's aspirations, the timely aspect of my research offered me optimism that my examinations could help the wider Armenian community and others who had felt culturally displaced through migration to feel empowered and celebrate their ethnic idiosyncrasies. From my experiences and dialogues with youthful and older Armenians, I recognised that the struggle to find some sort of belonging and placement was not uncommon for people of a diasporic culture, and although my investigations focused on these struggles of displacement and belonging from a performing arts perspective, I hoped that my discoveries and realisations could offer other Armenians in a similar position to mine parallel understandings of their ethnic identity in relation to their entire sense of Self. To help explore these relationships between identity as a director and identity as self, I considered the current literature available and interviewed respected contemporary theatre directors. In addition, I delved deeper into my reasons for becoming a theatre director to document conceivable links.

As a result, the research questions posed during the study were as follows:

1   How does theatre directing provide a sense of identity and belonging and potentially make explicit and, hence, in some way address the internal struggles an individual encounters through cultural displacement?

4 *Introduction*

2   Why was I attracted to the theatre?

   a) How does theatre facilitate and nurture my sense of identity and identity formation?
   b) What makes up identity and the search for self or both?

3   Why directing?

   a) How does theatre directing as a profession facilitate and nurture my sense of identity and identity formation?
   b) What are the experiences of other theatre directors who share a similar story?
   c) How does a sense of comfort, place, home, belonging and purpose in the theatre fulfil this role?

Accordingly, the study set out to explore these key methodological, theoretical and conceptual elements:

1   A methodology needed to be developed that would assist me in finding answers to these research inquiries. What practical techniques and methods would be employed, and how would the design of the study take form?
2   A deeper understanding towards the underlying characteristics of "the theatre" would help me understand what the history behind the space was and why I had been attracted to theatre as my chosen space of performance. Furthermore, what were the theatre's central qualities that no other creative medium offered that could be linked to an individual's exploration of self?
3   An investigation of identity and Self needed to be conducted so that I could ask what was identity and how was identity formed? What led to an individual's sense of displacement and how crucial was this displacement in the construction of that person's sense of self?
4   An honest investigation into my cultural disposition as a Persian-Armenian was required so that I could probe into my ethnic identity and culture. What were the personal reasons for my sense of cultural displacement that ultimately led me into the field of theatre directing? Acquiring a solid understanding of these three elements was fundamental to appreciating the contextual and theoretical knowledge that these areas encompassed.
5   Embarking on core phases of the research was the final step. Extensive investigations into the vocation of directing were conducted. While this period of examination ranged from the history of directing to the interviews and my immersion in the role of director, the primary function was to determine whether there were indeed links between the *director* and the *individual's* search for identity.

Structure of the book

Chapter 1, "Attracted to Theatre: Setting the Scene", is a discussion about what makes theatre unique and how it has remained such a prominent creative medium within our society through the ages. Why, as artists, do we continue to feel a need to keep creating within the discipline of theatre? Can theatre be a place where identities are played out and shaped and new ones formed? For this research, I specifically asked the following questions: Why does theatre appeal to my sense of identity (or its seeking), but more importantly, why did theatre directing become an avenue for my pursuits of seeking and forming identity?

Chapter 2, "Seeking Identity: Searching for Self", presents the theoretical framework in which the research is grounded. Within this chapter, I will discuss the philosophical basis for my investigations and how these underpinnings affected the course of my study, but more importantly, I situate my position as a researcher within the practice of directing. The theoretical framework provided me with insight into pre-existing knowledge developed by theorists and philosophers working in the areas of identity in direct correlation with my sense of cultural dislocation. The theoretical underpinnings offered here provided a focus for formulating my individual approach and suggest how these theories might offer insights into the links between cultural displacement and directing.

Chapter 3, "Affinity with Armenia: A Narrative in Two Parts", explores the history of Armenia and outlines why, as an Armenian, my allegiance to and, indeed, tussle with my cultural heritage has affected my life, both as an individual and a theatre director. I hope that this chapter not only provides some familiarity with Armenia as a nation but also, and more importantly, offers a deeper insight into my sense of being as a Persian-Armenian-Australian actor turned theatre director as I embarked on this intimate journey of self-discovery.

Chapter 4, "Dating Directing: Finding the Perfect Match", explores the vocation of directing and how the emergence of the director's role through history has developed within the medium of theatre. Within this chapter, I also explore the outcomes and discussions of the interviews conducted with the directors while examining the practical immersion of my work as a theatre director in relationship to the study. It was during this stage of my research that I began to question what attracts an individual to pursuing a path into directing and whether this pursuit has more to do with the individual's search for self and belonging than the mere finality of the play. Does directing as an authoritative creative outlet offer more incentives to the individual, and, if so, how does it do this and what are the individual's motivations?

Finally, in the conclusion, I make an attempt at summarising my findings within the research while inevitably leading to the deduction of how (re)discovery of identity takes place through the activity of directing. I will also give a brief yet personal account on how my own sense of (dis)placement, ipseity and assumptions of belonging were reimagined as a result of this study.

Methodology

The methodology that underpins this research is based on my understanding that there is no *one* way to exist within the world, but in fact, there are many ways. More often than not, individualistic behaviours are deeply influenced by the person's private history and social constraints, depending on where an individual may have come from. In *Multiple Realities*, Alfred Schuetz (1945) used psychologist

6 *Introduction*

William James's definition of this form of reality, stating, "The origin of all reality is subjective, whatever excites and stimulates our interest is real. To call a thing real means that this thing stands in a certain relation to ourselves" (p. 533). This particular way of thinking posits my understanding that there are multiple realities (or ways of thinking), which depend on a person's perceptions. An individual's insight constructs ways of knowing and receiving knowledge, which in turn affects the way that person absorbs and reflects this information. My level of understanding and awareness is deeply influenced by my social and political history and culture. As a researcher in the field of theatre directing, my ideas and ways of perceiving are directly influenced by these crucial components. The awareness and recognition of the cultural triangle of my cultural background and how that relates to my praxis as an actor turned director are paramount considerations that have continually evoked my practice.

These key theoretical and conceptual underpinnings are crucial in providing a solid understanding of directing but also of matters of identity. Therefore, my quest for the research structure that would best assist in uncovering this area of knowledge is a practice-led autoethnographical study into theatre directing.

Practice-led research

Practice-led research, as the term implies, is research that is led by the researcher's practice. This methodology is characteristically emergent, imagined and derivative of an artist or researcher's work and therefore capable of yielding outcomes that can be uniquely tailored towards that researcher's practice (Rolling, 2010), and it acknowledges the expertise of the researcher. In conjunction, theoretical and conceptual understandings surrounding identity and theatre directing supported the adoption of a practice-led research model. Using this model, I was able to take the embodied understandings that I had accumulated in my practice as a theatre director to help guide the investigations along the way. Because practice-led research is fundamentally concerned with the environment of the researcher's practice, it leads to new knowledge that holds importance for that particular field. More significantly, it calls upon the proficiencies, knowledge and work previously acquired by the researcher, which is then developed and honed throughout the course of the study.

Knowles and Cole (2008) outlined that "whether it is through poetry, prose, movement, drama, mime, meditation, painting, drawing, sculpture or any other non-traditional linguistic or non-linguistic form" (p. 63), the primary aim of creative research is to find a way or ways that will allow us to follow the natural internal flow of our own inquiry, through our understandings of art practice and research processes. Their thoughts on creative research reflect those of Brad Haseman (2006), who also suggested that the established research paradigms of quantitative and qualitative research do not resonate with practice-led researchers, and, therefore, new methodologies are required to help outline the distinct needs of creative research. Practice-led research as a methodological creative practice is a key element for unlocking these distinctive needs.

John Creswell (2002) asserted that one of the benefits of practice-led research, besides allowing the researcher to tailor the research uniquely towards a particular area of practice, is that it allows the researcher to conduct the study by employing a number of different methods in the exploration. This approach utilises multiple ways to explore a particular research problem. This multi-method approach has been described as bricolage, as articulated by Matt Rogers (2012). On par with Creswell (2002), Rogers asserted that bricolage can be considered a critical, multi-perspectival, multi-theoretical and multi-methodological approach to inquiry that allows an eclectic approach, which is fitting for creative research. Often as directors, we work with many ideas and points of inspiration, borrowing techniques and concepts from multiple sources.

In developing a practice-led model for my research, a strong framework was required – one that I could adapt and apply according to the requirements of the research. Haseman's (2006) practice-based categories, as outlined in *A Manifesto for Performative Research*, provided clear foundations and helped formulate the bricolage of methods that I applied to my study. The aspect of Haseman's strategy that stood out for me was his description of the reflective practitioner. He depicted a researcher who continually reflects "in-action and on-action" (p. 3). Haseman drew from philosopher Donald Schön's (1983) concept of the reflective practitioner and echoed that the advantage of this type of method was that it held "the capacity to reflect on action so as to engage in a process of continuous learning" (p. 102). Schön portrays the practitioner's reflection as operating almost as a corrective device to traditional overlearning and thus helping to generate new ideas and knowledge. He upheld that reflective practice is an important tool in practice-based professional learning as it assists with bringing together theory and practice. He articulated that, through rigorous reflection, practitioners can surface and critically unpack the tacit understandings that they had grown up with and around to in turn make sense of the situations of uncertainty and discovery around them.

Tacit knowledge

The recognition of tacit knowledge was an important aspect of my methodology because it played a significant role in my work as a theatre director. From my experience within the field of directing, I recognise that often there are occasions when, as a creative practitioner, I am required to make decisions or judgements in relation to my work. These "decisions", although appropriate to the task at the time, afterward cannot be articulated. They are knowledge, if you like, that is known, but it is difficult to express through spoken or written language. These decisions are often described as the instincts or hunches – the "know-hows" – that assist directors in making certain choices. Michael Polanyi (1967) dubbed these instincts the pre-logical phase or "tacit knowledge" – decisions that are motivated through our prior physical experiences of an event, which eventually with practice become tacit knowing. Polanyi observed that "we can know more than we can tell" (p. 4). These decisions range from informed guesses to the hunches or imaginings that form part of the stored repertoire of exploratory acts that individuals filter and then select from (Smith, 2003).

Tacit knowledge is heavily embedded within my work as a theatre director. The "informed guesses" I make are commonly recollections of lived experiences, whether successful or unsuccessful, that I have built up over time through my practice as a theatre director, both in Australia and overseas. Through trial and error, and over a variety of productions, I have learnt to recognise the elements in theatre that work better on stage, to the point where I do not need to deliberate over those decisions but, instead, can "instinctively" select a course of action because of my experience. I now recognise that these "instincts" or "hunches" are in fact not that at all, but they are grounded within the practised elements of knowledge that I have accumulated over the years.

In a study conducted by researchers Irit Alony and Michael Jones (2007), the notion of tacit knowledge was explored within the field of performing arts and entertainment. Alony and Jones revealed that many of the professionals whom they interviewed stated that, within the (performing arts/entertainment) industry, first-hand accumulated experience is often far more important than qualifications. These findings resonate with the research of leading experts Ikujio Nonaka and Hirotaka Takeuchi (1995), who outlined that tacit knowledge encompasses the "subjective insights, intuitions, and hunches" (p. 8) that are deeply rooted in the action, experience, ideals, values and emotions that the individual embraces. Further, they held that these critical elements are often hard to interpret or replicate.

Autoethnography and reflexivity

According to Reed-Danahay (1997), autoethnography can be defined as "a self-narrative that critiques the situatedness of self with others in social contexts. Autoethnography is both a method and a text of diverse interdisciplinary praxes" (as cited in Spry, 2001, p. 710). For my work as a director-researcher, the advantage of utilising this technique was that I was able to examine critically all facets of "myself" through each aspect of the research. My research was initiated by a curiosity about the possible links between cultural displacement and directing; an autoethnographical approach meant that the research was not bound to the traditional conventions of academic writing and research. Instead of separating the research from the researcher, I was able to draw upon my ethnic identity and my expertise as a theatre director to express the research on a more personal level.

Carolyn Ellis and Arthur Bochner (2000) explained that an "autobiographical genre of writing and research is one that displays multiple layers of consciousness, connecting the personal to the cultural" (p. 739). Authors of *Handbook of Qualitative Research* Denzin and Lincoln (2000) agree and claimed that this approach is "self-reflective, introspective, observant, and self-questioning in ethnography of the self. The researcher, too, becomes subject, turning our observations back on ourselves" (p. 747). This autoethnographical approach was tailored to the multi-model research, allowing for a more personal approach to the research and to the collection of data. For example, when interviewing the directors, I compared their experiences to mine to determine whether they included similar events.

As an autoethnographical researcher, it was critical that I recognised the application of reflexivity. John Creswell stated, "Reflexivity in research is meant to trace the presence of the researcher onto the research context, marking their interference, their participation and their desire" (as cited in Knowles & Cole, 2008, p. 4). In the research, the context of identity and directing was initiated by the trace of my own motivations for pursuing a career in theatre directing and that deep desire to uncover and understand how a culturally displaced individual can find a sense of identity and self through the profession. Initially, I sought to discover whether my suspicions had any significant footing or whether they were based purely on my personal experience.

In *Lives and Legacies: A Guide to Qualitative Interviewing*, Hsiung (2010) noted that "reflexivity involves making the research process itself a focus of inquiry, laying open pre-conceptions and becoming aware of situational dynamics in which the interviewer and respondent are jointly involved in knowledge production" (Why Be Reflexive section, para. 3). Reflexivity was palpable during the interview sessions, as the directors and I were jointly involved and responsive to the idea of knowledge production. At the same time, I was aware that the information that I was receiving from my respondents could be subjected to my interpretations of the data. That is not to say that I deliberately sought to manipulate the data; however, subjectivity and bias are always present within research, in the choice of questions and the researcher's control of the interviews, as well as in the later interpretation and analyses of the responses.

Although reflexivity may sound neat and tidy on paper, my experience was quite the opposite. Reflexivity raised awareness of the chaos and messiness that often exists within autoethnographical research. In fact, as Catherine (2010) noted, reflexivity acknowledges the difficult position of researchers because they are aware of the innumerable issues that may affect a study, which makes it difficult for them to remain unbiased. This un-bias or transparency is an imperative ingredient of any study, not only because of the ethical considerations that must be taken into account when embarking on a project but more importantly because of the study's dependence on the researcher's self-awareness. Reflexivity constantly prompts the researcher to be conscious of the cultural, political, social, linguistic and ideological influences on perception (Catherine, 2010). Catherine also warned that the process of reflexivity, which involves the self-questioning and self-understanding that are obligatory for an autoethnographical study, can be confronting. By acknowledging the subjectivity, interpretation and interference that existed, my understanding of reflexivity strengthened and brought ethical considerations into my focus as a researcher, *for* the study, *into* the study and *through* the study (Frayling, 1993, p. 8), both for the participants and for the material itself.

The interviews

The interviews were pivotal to my study as they were the core element in uncovering new insights in the area of theatre directing, in itself a "hidden" creative art form. This means that to gain understanding of the profession one has to be in the rehearsal room with the director or to ask the directors forthrightly their discernments about the role. Therefore, not only did the interviews play a vital role in the discovery of new comprehensions of and insights into the director's role, but they also provided newfound considerations of the research questions. While these new queries addressed my original suspicions, they also led me to new areas I had not imagined before. The first phase of the interviews, via the answers received from the directors, fundamentally assisted in formulating the rest of the work. Knowles and Cole's (2008) *Handbook of the Arts in Qualitative Research* highlights the importance of the act of interviewing that requires intense attentiveness to the other's voice, which is at the core of a collaborative research process. Carter McNamara (1999) believes that "interviews are particularly useful for getting the story behind a participant's experiences. The interviewer can pursue in-depth information around a topic" (Introduction section, para. 1). Before I could begin unravelling the mystery and elusive nature of directing, gaining perceptions from current directors and delving into the profession through their understandings and reasons for pursuing this career path would significantly inform the research.

I conducted the interviews with the directors by asking them open-ended questions that would lead to discussion and provide insight into their personal views surrounding the role. Open-ended questions, as suggested by Michael Patton (2001), "yield in-depth responses about people's experiences, perceptions, opinion, feelings, and knowledge. Data consists of verbatim quotations with sufficient context to be interpretable" (p. 14). I accepted Patton's suggestions about how to conduct the interview sessions and what they should yield, and as a result, the responses that I received from the directors formed several of the more fundamental discoveries I made in my study, as discussed in Chapter 4, "Dating Directing: Finding the Perfect Match".

The interviews were conducted over two phases with particular selections of theatre directors. The process behind choosing which directors to interview stemmed from my curiosity about whether there was, indeed, a link between an individual's sense of cultural displacement and directing. I began by interviewing professional directors from culturally diverse backgrounds – both in Australia and overseas. I defined culturally diverse directors as those who do not identify with being first-generation citizens of the country in which they are residing, either through birth or through migration. This marked Phase 1 of the interviews. The breakthroughs I made during this phase, although unexpected and encouraging, cemented my initial postulations; there was something more there to be explored (discussed in Chapter 4, "Dating Directing: Finding the Perfect Match"). In Phase 2, I selected a new group of directors, which included a few of the directors from Phase 1. During this selection phase, the cultural backgrounds of the directors were not as pivotal. Instead, in this phase, I was interested in what was unique about the director's journey. During Phase 1, 12 directors were interviewed, whereas Phase 2 consisted of 10 participants. In both phases, directors were interviewed until the point of saturation. By that I mean directors were interviewed until the collection of new data did not shed any further light on the issue under investigation (Glaser & Strauss, 1999). I have intertwined the findings from these interviews within the book at various points to either support or challenge my discoveries. Full interview questions and lists of all directors interviewed from Phases 1 and 2 of the interviews are presented in the Appendix.

In summary

Many of the underlying elements of this study originated from my own narrative as a displaced individual with a confused sense of self. These various suspicions led me on a path to examine and re-examine the links between my sense of identity as a Persian-Armenian-Australian and my role as an actor turned theatre director. Subconsciously, by being immersed in my directing practice, I had already embarked on this journey of self-identification and rediscovery. As far back as I can remember, I have been in pursuit of individual artistic clarity and vision as a director in Australia but also in pursuit of an innate clarity into who I am as an individual and where I belong. What I strove for via this research was to redefine my journey because, although it may have begun long ago, its destination was yet and, in fact, is yet to be discovered. As someone who struggled with identity and belonging most of my adolescent and adult life, I trust that, viscerally, my quest for reflective awareness of this matter led me into the creative path of directing. Through the following chapters, I explore and communicate the idiosyncratic links between identity and directing through a more intimate and innovative understanding that will offer new insight into these often subjective areas.

References

Alony, I., & Jones, M. (2007). *Tacit Knowledge, explicability and creativity: A study of the Australian film industry*. University of Wollongong, Research Online.
Catherine. (2010). *Reflexivity*. Retrieved from http://reflectionsofgoodqualitativeresearch. blogspot.com.au/2011/02/reflexivity.html
Cole, S. L. (1992). *Directors in rehearsal: A hidden world*. New York: Routledge.
Cole, T., & Chinoy, H.-K. (1953). *Directors on directing: A source book of the modern theatre*. London: Peter Owen Limited.
Creswell, J. W. (2002). *Research design, qualitative, quantitative and mixed methods approaches* (2nd ed.). Thousand Oaks, CA: Sage Publications.
Denzin, N. K., & Lincoln, Y. S. (Eds.). (2000). *Handbook of qualitative research* (2nd ed.). Thousand Oaks, CA: Sage Publications.
Ellis, C., & Bochner, A. P. (2000). Autoethnography, personal narrative, reflectivity: Researcher as subject. In N. Denzin & Y. Lincoln (Eds.), *The handbook of qualitative research* (pp. 733–768). Thousand Oaks, CA: Sage Publications.
Evans, B. (1987, January 9). The lonely stage of life. *The Sydney Morning Herald*.
Frayling, C. (1993). Research in art and design. *Royal College of Art Research Papers*, *1*(1).
Glaser, B. G., & Strauss, A. L. (1999). *The discovery of grounded theory: Strategies for qualitative research*. New Brunswick, NJ and New York: Aldine Transaction.
Haseman, B. (2006). Media International Australia incorporating culture and policy, theme issue "practice-led research". *A Manifesto for Performative Research, QUT RePrints*, no. 118, 98–106.

Hsiung, P. C. (2010). Lives and legacies: A guide to qualitative interviewing. *Reflexivity*. Retrieved from www.utsc.utoronto.ca/~pchsiung/LAL/reflexivity

Knowles, J. G., & Cole, A. L. (2008). *Handbook of the arts in qualitative research: Perspectives, methodologies, examples, and issues*. Thousand Oaks, CA: Sage Publications.

McNamara, C. (1999). *General guidelines for conducting interviews*. Retrieved from https://fye.uconn.edu/wp-content/uploads/sites/435/2017/04/Handout-Tips-for-Conducting-Research-Interviews.docx

Nonaka, I., & Takeuchi, H. (1995). *The knowledge-creating company: How Japanese companies create the dynamics of innovation*. New York: Oxford University Press.

Patton, M. (2001). *Qualitative evaluation and research methods*. London: Sage Publications.

Polanyi, M. (1967). *The tacit dimension*. New York: Anchor Books.

Reed-Danahay, D. (1997). *Auto/ethnography: Rewriting the self and the social (explorations in anthropology)*. London: Bloomsbury Academic.

Rogers, M. (2012). Contextualizing theories and practices of bricolage research. *The Qualitative Report, 17*(7), 1–17.

Rolling Jr., J. H. (2010). A paradigm analysis of arts-based research and implications for education. *National Art Education Association Studies in Art Education: A Journal of Issues and Research, 51*, 102–114.

Schön, D. (1983). *The reflective practitioner, how professionals think in action*. New York: Ingram Publisher Services US.

Schuetz, A. (1945). On multiple realities. *Philosophy and Phenomenological Research, 5*(4), 533–576.

Smith, M. K. (2003). *Michael Polanyi and tacit knowledge*. Retrieved from http://infed.org/mobi/michael-polanyi-and-tacit-knowledge/

Spry, T. (2001). Performing autoethnography: An embodied methodological praxis. *Qualitative Inquiry, 7*(6), 706–732.

Squires, N. (2015, February 6). Amal Clooney takes on Armenia Genocide case in European court. *The Telegraph*. Retrieved from www.telegraph.co.uk/news/worldnews/europe/armenia/11341003/Amal-Clooney-takes-on-Armenia-genocide-case-in-European-court.html

Tufankjian, S. (2014). *The Armenian Diaspora Project*. Retrieved from www.kickstarter.com/projects/303104019/the-armenian-diaspora-project

Tufankjian, S. (2015). *There is only the earth: Images from the Armenian Diaspora Project*. New York: Melcher Media.

Ward, P. (1988). The Whiz of Les Misérables. An interview with Australian theatre director Gale Edwards. *The Australian*, pp. 11–12.

1 Attracted to theatre: setting the scene

> The stage is a magic circle where only the most real things happen, a neutral territory outside the jurisdiction of Fate where stars may be crossed with impunity. A truer and more real place does not exist in all the universe.
>
> (Baber, 2010, p. 204)

Prologue

At the age of 7, my father cast me in an Armenian play he was directing called *The Dog and the Cat*. I was to play the cat. He had adapted the play from a poem by acclaimed Armenian writer Hovhannes Tumanyan. When I think back to this experience, I remember the overwhelming responsibility of having to learn lines and deliver them on cue every night. Feelings of anxious excitement and not wanting to let my father down envelop my memory. For over a decade, my father was an influential theatre director and practitioner in Iran. In 1969, he gave up his final year of studying architecture at a prestigious university to attend the first ever drama school built in the country called the Institute of Dramatic Arts. In 1979, he emerged as one of the few pioneering graduates who had completed the three-year degree. Even upon coming to Australia, my father continued to be dedicated to his professional career, working as a film technician and theatre director in both the cinematic and performing arts industries. While my father's creative pursuits may have influenced my decisions, as we seemed to follow a similar path, possibly as an Armenian living under the strict regime of an Iranian government and then as a migrant Australian, my father suffered from a sense of cultural displacement, which may have influenced his decisions. Little did I know that the experience at the age of 7 would be life altering. From that moment on, I knew I needed to be "in the theatre". Therefore, in spite of my mother's disapproval, I too made the unorthodox decision to defer my university studies in psychology and audition for the Australian Academy of Dramatic Art in Sydney. Several years later, I again left my mother distraught when I departed the comforts of my home in Sydney, Australia, to study at the Atlantic Theater Company Acting School in New York. As terrified as I was and as cliché as it sounds, it was as if I had no choice in the matter. I was drawn by the need to explore more deeply my creative instincts in the milieu of the theatre. An uncertainty has remained with me ever since. Why the explicit attraction to the theatre?

The essence of theatre

Records of dramatic conception and theatrical performance have co-existed since the time of ancient Greeks and continued during medieval Europe, Tudor England and the France of Louis XIV (Cole & Chinoy, 1953, p. 4). According to Robert Cohen (2011, 2013), the word "theatre" is derived from the Greek word *teatron*, or seeing place, but no one knows as a certainty the origins of theatre. We can assume that, like most of civilisation, it arose from Africa via rituals and storytelling traditions. However, although debate surrounding the origins of theatre may vary, it is also important to note that the discussion depends on whether the chosen standpoint is an Eastern or Western cultural perspective (Cohen, 2013). For the purposes of this study, predominantly a Western theorists' perspective on theatre was favoured.

With that being the case, there are numerous texts that offer an overview of what theatre's purpose was *imagined* to be (Cole & Chinoy, 1953). In the distant past, theatre was used more as a way to help express the ritualistic ways of daily life by creating stories and myths that people could reflect upon and live by. Antonin Artaud, a French theatre director and playwright in the early twentieth century, held a belief that theatre should represent reality and affect the audience as much as possible. As theatre was representative of daily ritualistic life, he championed this "involvement" for both performer and audience as desiring to remove aesthetic distance by bringing the audience into direct contact with the dangers of life (Miall & Kuiken, 1994). In this way, he thought audiences would become involved with the action of the theatre and, as a result, would experience theatre (and in turn life) in all its pleasure and cruelty:

> The theatre must make itself the equal of life – not an individual life, that individual aspect of life in which CHARACTERS [*sic*] triumph, but the sort of liberated which sweeps away human individuality and in which man is only a reflection. The true purpose of the theatre is to create Myths, to express life in its immense, universal aspects, and from that life to extract images in which we find pleasure in discovering ourselves.
>
> (Artaud, 1958, p. 116)

It is evident that, no matter its use, for centuries, theatre has offered an outlet to people by "providing an occasion for a social gathering, with performances that demonstrate unpalatable truths in flesh that can awaken common responses among a large number of people" (Brown, 1997, p. 6).

Theatrical storytelling, formulated by the Greeks, evolved through history into what we recognise as Western theatre in its present form. John Russell Brown (1997) explored theatre in-depth and presented the idea that theatre has been many things: "Theatre can be a social art form, a lively powerful means of sharing ideas with thousands of people, and as a result has been subjected to severe political censorship in certain places and at certain times" (pp. 5–6). Paul Kuritz (1988), for instance, took the powerful nature of theatre and extended it to its origins of myth and ritual. According to Kuritz, "The peculiar distinguishing features of the special kind of theatre that interests us reveal themselves when myth and ritual are viewed as the progenitors of theatre" (p. 3). Dave Kelman and Jane Rafe (2011) extended Kuritz's explorations of myth and ritual and examined how mythology has been used in a theatrical way in primary education. They said that the accessibility of this device through dramatic expression enables young people to develop a critical awareness as a channel for generating the contemporary meaning of issues within their own lives. Kelman and Rafe (2011) believe that the pivotal point here is that the process of translation of the ideas from one symbolic language to another inherently becomes integrated into the work and, therefore, myth becomes a vehicle for individuals generating deep understanding of their own human experience(s). They went on to elaborate that "meaning like all meaning – is specific to its context, but it emerges from a process in which young people are developing moral reasoning and creating their own sense of order in the world" (p. 11). Through Kelman and Rafe's (2011) examples, we begin to notice that it is not so much theatre as a *form* (the result) that seems to hold all the influence. Instead, it is the *essence* in which theatre is created (the process) that allows for the change, the self-awareness and the expression of ideas.

American theatre director Anne Bogart (2001) memorably said, "I regard the theatre as an art form because I believe in its transformative power" (p. 1). In uncomplicated terms, theatre is "the activity or profession of acting in, producing, directing, or writing plays, in a building or outdoor area in which plays and other dramatic performances are given" (Pearsall & Hanks, 2010). I do not disagree with this definition, although theatre means much more to me personally than simply an activity resulting in a performance. I agree with Bogart's notion of the uniquely transformative power of theatre, whose intimate and synergetic processes enable its personnel (performers, playwrights and designers) to come together and visually represent a story to a live audience in an imaginatively charged place, which is scarcely available via any other medium.

Throughout history, evidence suggests that theatre and its origins in rituals have been constant in most, if not all, societies. Debra Bruch (1990) believes that the reason for theatre's permanency transcends myth and ritual and may have something to do with its innate ability for storytelling. Bruch stated,

> Unlike any other art, the total, intense focus of theatre is on the human being, his or her existence, and his or her relationship with life. It is a part of human nature to need to examine who we are in relationship with where we are.
> (p. 1)

From the very beginning, societies have used storytelling as conventions to help explain human life. For the most part, these stories have assisted human beings in understanding their relationships with their environments and helped individuals and groups to understand their own natures (Bruch, 1990). William Shakespeare wrote stories that were reflective of the society in which he lived. Even today, Shakespeare's plays are the most performed throughout the English-speaking world. According to *On Shakespeare and His Times* (Cannon et al., 2009), the longevity of Shakespeare's work can be attributed to his "keen eye for detail and his sharp understanding of human nature, which enabled him to create some of the most enduring works of drama and poetry ever produced" (p. 5).

Artaud considered that the practice of theatre "wakes us up: nerves and heart", through which we experience "violent action". In turn, that action inspires us with the "fiery magnetism of its images and acts upon us like a spiritual therapeutics whose touch can never be forgotten" (as cited in Gorelick, 2011, p. 263). Is this need for theatre that Artaud proclaimed due to the substance and processes of the art form itself, or is it due to a core human desire to portray and express *our* stories?

In 2012, several theatre makers posted blogs on what theatre meant to them and why theatre was an essential part of society today. Rena Cherry Brown (2012) considered that theatre emerged because

> in hard times people need to gather in one place, to be lifted, challenged or simply entertained. To experience a communal energy of emotion, wonder, fascination, brilliance, commentary. This is not a luxury, it is essential to being a human being.
>
> (para. 1)

Although Brown's opinion regarding the permanence of theatre is articulate and corresponds with my outlook, the elucidation that resonated most with me came from the artistic director of the Hub Theatre in Washington, Helen Pafumi (2012). She observed that theatre has a transitory spiritual aspect that other creative mediums rarely convey. Pafumi (2012) understood theatre as an "electric juncture" that allows the audience to "breathe in the same air" as the story transports from "living being to living being". Once that "fleeting instant is over", theatre then becomes "'our' [the audience's] shared chronicle" (para. 8). What both authors communicate are the rare transformational and communal aspects of the theatre that allow participatory immersion into the story.

With this in mind, I began to look at my specific motivations for pursuing a profession in the theatre. I wondered how theatre's performative power might have assisted my considerations surrounding the deep struggles I had with my identity and, in essence, my "order in the world" (Kelman & Rafe, 2011, p. 11). What makes theatre distinctive and how has it remained such a prominent creative medium through the ages? Moreover, why do performing artists continue to feel a need to create within the discipline of theatre? Could theatre be a place where identities are played out and shaped and new ones formed? More importantly, how is it that the theatre as a performing arts convention and the decision to become a director encompass so much of my identity as an individual? The answer may lie within the individual's attraction to the theatre as a sociological phenomenon. To understand theatre from a sociological perspective, as well as its location in the wider community, I turned to Bourdieu (1977, 1984) to unpack the conundrum between individual agency and the pressures of social formation.

Theatre as a social construct

Arguably, each production of a play for the theatre can, in itself, be seen as a microcosm of society for the participants in that production. There is a space where an event takes place, a sense of community that develops whereby members either actively or inactively partake in its action, and to finish (for the most part), there is a response, celebration or engagement that results in some form of a debrief. It is, therefore, imaginable that theatre is a social experience that relies on individuals within that society or community to come together to perform or present a story for others within that community. French theorist Pierre Bourdieu (1977) used the term "cultural practices" for all types of activities played out within societies. Bourdieu devised a "generic category for art in order to identify art [the arts] as a cultural activity, hence also a social one" (as cited in Shevtsova, 2002, p. 36). For Bourdieu, creative (or any other) industries, such as the theatre, can be understood as fields of artistic production. In his view, society is defined by what he called "the social room", and within each room, there is a "field" linked to its own specific practice and, as a result, operating via its own set of rules. Bourdieu argued that the rules need to be respected at all times by the "agents" (i.e. the individuals involved in the field). An agent's position within the field can shift or strengthen, depending on the value that individual accrues within the field. He called these "battles" or "negotiations" between an individual and the field's rules "playing the game". Further, Bourdieu (1977) added that individuals do not have to belong to that specific field to subscribe to it, but they do need to be agents of it to contribute discussions on the value of that field's position.

If we apply Bourdieu's (1977) idea to a rehearsal room in a theatre, we can say that within the rehearsal room are its agents. These are the actors, the director, possibly the playwright, and the technical crew. They are the agents (players) with "value" within that field. Therefore, as long as they respect the rules, they can play the game to strengthen their positions. The actors can play against each other to have their opinions considered, as can the director and the designers, and so on. However, Bourdieu (1977) advised that the players within the field have their particular "distinctions" or rankings of class. Therefore, while in the rehearsal room, all of the agents can partake in the game, there is an obvious hierarchy to which they must adhere. Directors, for the most part, have the highest position, so they have more influence or, as Bourdieu would say, the most value within that field. Bourdieu viewed his *field theory* as a microcosm of the greater society, and inside it, we all sense and play a particularly idiosyncratic game. By adopting Bourdieu's *field theory* and using the theatre as a small-scale version of the wider community or society, we can look deeper into theatrical conventions and begin to assess the rules governing the theatre's "players".

Social groups are characterised by the individuals within that group. Inside that social construct, the members are endowed with social ranks, duties and responsibilities within which their individual identities are shaped, both in relationship to her/himself and towards the other members within that community. In an interview, French actress Juliette Binoche said, "Choosing to be in the theatre was a way to put my roots down somewhere with other people. It was a way to choose a new family" (as cited in Grimm, French, & Pak, 2014, para. 3). In the theatre, individuals are rarely alone; instead, they are part of a group, or as Binoche proposed, "a family". Following Bourdieu, let us accept that inside the theatre, there are various individuals, all of whom have numerous duties and accountabilities that are distinctive depending on each person's specific role. An individual's sense of identity, then, relies on another person's position in the game and, rapidly, all these "identities" become enmeshed in association and negotiation with each other. As the director is considered at the top of the hierarchy, in turn, this status affects the director's interrelations with the other members of the group.

Within the role of the director, individuals also have the capacity to shape their personal *ipseity*, which uniquely characterises their identity within that role. Ipseity is a word derived from the Latin "self" that means "selfhood; individual identity, individuality" (Pearsall & Hanks, 2010). Although this word is seldom used within the English language, at times I purposely use it in my thesis, as I find it an astute demonstration of the multiple facets that make up an individual's identity because it encompasses both the personality and the cultural framework of that individual. Often, directors that I interviewed said that they believed theatre was full of misfits and outcasts, who somehow come together and find acceptance and a sense of community within the constructs of the field. Theatre practitioner/ educator Nicole Cervonaro said,

> *When an individual who has felt outcast or lost finally finds purpose and direction [in the theatre], it creates a strong sense of identity. For many directors, particularly theatre directors, the process is not solitary and often, for both cast and crew, a sense of belonging to a family develops.*
>
> (Interview, 23 March 2014)

Similarly, Yoti Lane, the author of *The Psychology of the Actor* (1960), noted that, commonly, these are people who have felt some form of segregation from the social rooms within their lives as a result of "an aggressive society which can be violent and punitive in its reactions to disobedience or nonconformity, yet benign when its demands are met" (p. 39). The theatre offers a place where prejudices, for the most part, are abandoned. As such, individuals who have experienced some form of rejection come together in a supportive setting and are able to begin formulating their own sense of self in a relatively non-judgemental situation. Lane's understanding of the actor's psyche may go some way to explaining some individuals' attraction to the theatre. Lane explained,

> Because of the difference between the actor's basic emotional pattern and that of the non-actor, the actor becomes conscious of his separateness from

society early in his life. His awareness of this psychological chasm may first arise when he timidly voices his desire for a theatrical career.

(p. 42)

When I began to reflect upon my journey into a career in theatre, Lane's (1960) analysis of the psychological awareness of difference between the *actor* and the *non-actor* became thought provoking. If an individual's identity has been disparaged in the formative years and seemingly not much interest has been shown towards that person's narrative, then, unexpectedly, the *theatre* can provide a unique space where that individual is given permission to explore the multifaceted possibilities of who s/he is. I consider this a crucial element of theatre; for in an environment such as this, suddenly, the individual's story is given value, and thus who you are and where you have come from begins to matter in a positive sense. A space or place is established where displaced individuals find commonalities with other displaced individuals, and a sense of family and community can be developed.

The theatre and me

In Armenian, we have a word, Ճակատագիր,[1] which means "written on the forehead", referring to one's fate or destiny. Armenians believe that every person is born with this Ճակատագիր, meaning that their fate and purpose in life are already predetermined. This is an understanding or way of existing that is deeply ingrained within us. Whenever a major obstacle or event occurred, my mother would say, "There is no point in worrying about it; whatever is meant to happen will happen; *that* is your Ճակատագիր". This understanding of Ճակատագիր does not mean that individuals do not pursue a path of becoming the type of person they aspire to be or forge a career in whichever field their passions lead them. It simply means that while individuals are on that path of becoming, that numinous path may have already been selected for them. The reason I raise this understanding is that I cannot for the life of me remember if I made a "choice" to pursue a path in the theatre or whether my decision was predestined by my Ճակատագիր. More importantly, how did the theatre as a performing arts convention and the decision to become a director encompass so much of my identity as an individual?

Who I am or where I came from was rarely scrutinised in my workplaces to the extent to which theatre has dissected me as an individual. In my various places of work, rarely did people need to know about my personal underpinnings. Generally, in delivering my work, I was required to be on time and deliver it well; my individual identity mostly remained superfluous. In the theatre, it is different. Not only do people show interest in who I am or where I came from but also the transparency of my "story" is obligatory to enhancing my artistic credibility. It seems that this is not uncommon. In the theatre, unique personalities tend to be prized. Theatre greats Constantin Stanislavski (1937, 1958, 1962), Antonin Artaud (1958; Hirschman, 2001) and Jerzy Grotowski (Grotowski & Barba, 2002) have sought to highlight the importance of actors' differentiated qualities by requesting that they probe deeper into what makes them uniquely the individuals they are, both emotionally and psychologically.

The early 1900s marked a crucial stage of change in theatrical history with the introduction of realist and naturalist playwrights. An example is Russian playwright Anton Chekhov, who moved theatre away from the melodramatic façade of presentational theatre into a new phase of realistic storytelling and acting (Rayfield, 1998). Working closely with Chekhov, Stanislavski played a pivotal role within this movement and, through his fascination with the psychological realities of the characters within a play, understood that acting had to present believable behaviour for an audience (Moore, 1965). Although there is much debate over whether Stanislavski's work did in fact create a system or "method", over time, texts have been presented as the "Stanislavski Method" (David, 2011; Sawoski, 2012). According to past students of Stanislavski who began documenting his training early on, initially, Stanislavski focused on the empathic observation of people in various situations. Through this acute attention to the observation of others, he discovered that a wide range of emotional actions and reactions can be developed onstage, which will make actors appear as if they were a part of the real world rather than a make-believe one (Stanislavski, as cited in Moore, 1965). This in turn makes the characters look more representational of "real life". Accordingly, Stanislavski (1962) determined that for actors to portray the utmost truth of a character and be as realistic as possible, they need to embark on a process of strenuous artistic and individualistic self-analysis and reflection.

Artaud equally understood that for actors to be boundless and as truthful as possible, they need to "act out" (as cited in Bermel, 2001, p. 104) their fears and insecurities by exploring deep within their underlying foundations as human beings. For Artaud, this act was potentially cathartic and endowed the actor and, in turn, the audience, with an uninhibited theatrical experience. Similarly, Polish theatre director Jerzy Grotowski was fascinated with the actor's selfhood (Davis & Postlewait, 2003). On the first page of *Towards a Poor Theatre*, Grotowski stated in bold print, "We consider the personal and scenic technique of the actor as the core of theatre art" (Grotowski & Barba, 2002, p. 15). Grotowski was intensely interested in archetypes and the human condition and extended Artaud's understandings by creating an environment similar to that of a laboratory where actors were encouraged to unpack their identities and behavioural traits down to their very essences. Therefore, when combined, Stanislavski's, Artaud's and Grotowski's ideas about acting have often been compared to that of psychoanalysis (Meyer-Dinkgrafe, 2001). Although the three luminaries developed their theatrical explorations with actors in diverse ways, all shared a belief that the personal underpinnings of actors as individual human beings are vital and warrant in-depth analysis. This mindset and theatrical framework for the actor has largely prevailed and paved the way for performers in theatre today.

Reconciling ideas such as *belonging* and the *in-between* is undoubtedly never easy or simplistic. For my part, I imagine that the emotions of not belonging, which followed me continuously throughout my adolescence, were due to the multiplicity of my identities, being somehow connected to all, yet truly belonging to none. In regard to the *in-between*, I imagine my feelings were provoked by a deep longing to be acknowledged as a genuine "Aussie". I felt denigrated because of my racial underpinnings, so I grew up resenting my Armenian inheritance. Within the Armenian community, whether it was at Saturday school, scouts or folk dancing, I wilfully positioned myself as an outsider. I never gave myself permission to enjoy any of the cultural pleasures that the rest of the Armenians seemed to share. In my mind, it was this culture that had made me so dissimilar to the common stereotypical representation of an Australian. For that reason, while I felt "Australia" was positioning me as an outsider within its community, I was positioning myself as an outsider within my Armenian community, hence segregating myself from both cultures.

In the theatre, however, none of my cultural anxieties mattered. Indeed, being "the other" (Bhabha, 1983) became rather interesting, and my individual story as the migrant Armenian unexpectedly gained traction. The social stigmas attached to the *other* rapidly began to fade, and through theatre, I was able to reinvent myself. Sanjoy Ganguly (2011) explained that theatre is "a space for introspection and collective action. A space where politics in the form of a collective action is complemented by spirituality in the form of introspection . . . theatre is hope, theatre is freedom" (p. 97). Of course, I understand this concept of Ganguly's is filled with varying complexities; however, it made me wonder if the ideas surrounding theatre as a vehicle for nonconformity and freedom of opinions serve as an incentive for individuals perplexed by their cultural identities. Perhaps the nonconformity and freedom of expression are, in fact, part of the "rules of the game" (Bourdieu, 1977) for its performers. From here, directly or indirectly, working in the theatre seems to assist individuals in coming to terms with who they are in some shape or form. During the interviews, several theatre makers and directors discussed having similar experiences and acknowledged their own personal struggles with their cultural identities. Most, if not all, offered similar comments on what they believe is unique about theatre and the performing arts in general. These comments for the large part concerned the process of theatre, the relationships created within it and the freedom the forum allows for individual explorations of self-identity. Cervonaro again observed that,

> *It [theatre] is like no other industry as it forces you to put your entire self on display, making you connect with others in a short span of time and relationships develop intensely. It is the connection, the intensity of the work, the speed at which the process progresses, that is addictive. It's just like a family. A sense of belonging to a family develops through this united process.*
> (Interview, 23 March 2014)

Cervonaro's words and outlook regarding the unique nature that theatre presents to its participants (both the actors and the creative staff) within its configurations were echoed throughout the group of directors I interviewed. Theatre being described as a powerful vessel that allows people to explore their identities may be due to a combination of factors: the stories that are explored, the community or sense of family that develops within the working relationships and the unique nature of the space (the theatre) itself as a place to play out endless possibilities in an unrestrictive, imaginative and often forbearing environment. Bourdieu (1977) described this *essence* of the space as a social experience that relies on individuals within the social room to come together and perform or present a story as a unified company. As such, one individual's sense of identity relies on another person's position within the team and rapidly, all these identities suddenly become enmeshed in association and negotiation with each other. Through these negotiations, the individuals begin to explore their particular sense of self and purpose. In the process, a unique sense of ipseity is developed and nurtured, but more importantly, it is encouraged.

Note

1 Ճակատագիր, pronounced *ja-ka-ta-gir*.

References

Artaud, A. (1958). *The theater and its double*. New York: Grove Press, Inc.
Baber, P. S. (2010). *Cassie draws the universe*. iUniverse.com.
Bermel, A. (2001). *Artaud's theatre of cruelty*. New York: Bloomsbury Methuen Drama.
Bhabha, H. K. (1983). The other question, the stereotype and colonial discourse. *Oxford Journals*, 24(6), 18–36.
Bogart, A. (2001). *A director prepares: Seven essays on art and theatre*. London: Routledge.
Bourdieu, P. (1977). *An outline of a theory of practice*. Cambridge: Cambridge University Press.
Bourdieu, P. (1984). *Distinction: A social critique of the judgement of taste*. Cambridge, MA: Harvard University Press.
Brown, J. R. (1997). *What is theatre? An introduction and exploration*. Oxford: Butterworth-Heinemann.
Brown, R. C. (2012). Essential to being human. *theatreWashington*. Retrieved from http://theatrewashington.org/content/essential-being-human
Bruch, D. (1990). Directing theatre. *Debra Bruch*. Retrieved from http://dbruch.hypermart.net/engineer/direct.html
Cannon, J., Edwards, L., Limber, C., Neiman, A. M., Perkins, M. B., & Valdes, J. (2009). *On Shakespeare and his times*. Retrieved from www.sfstl.com/wp-content/uploads/2013/07/On-Shakespeare-and-His-Times.pdf
Cohen, R. (2011). *Working together in theatre: Collaboration and leadership*. Thousand Oaks, CA: Palgrave Macmillan.
Cohen, R. (2013). *Theatre: Brief version* (10th ed.). New York: McGraw-Hill Humanities/Social Sciences/Languages.
Cole, T., & Chinoy, H.-K. (1953). *Directors on directing: A source book of the modern theatre*. London: Peter Owen Limited.
David, J. (2011). Twenty-first-century Russian actor training: Active analysis in the UK. *Theatre, Dance and Performance Training*, 2(2), 166.
Davis, T. C., & Postlewait, T. (2003). *Theatricality*. London: Cambridge University Press.

Ganguly, S. (2011). Theatre is hope, theatre is freedom. In S. Schonmann (Ed.), *Key concepts in theatre/drama education*. Rotterdam, The Netherlands: Sense Publishers.

Gorelick, N. (2011). Life and excess: Insurrection and expenditure in Antonin Artaud's theatre of cruelty. *Project Muse, 33*(2), 263–279.

Grimm, L., French, L., & Pak, E. (2014). *Juliette Binoche biography*. Retrieved from Bio. A&E Television Networks www.biography.com/people/juliette-binoche-9212900#awesm=~oGF6BRpMJeqsyx

Grotowski, J., & Barba, E. (2002). *Towards a poor theatre*. New York: Routledge.

Hirschman, J. (2001). *Artaud anthology*. San Francisco: City Lights Publishers.

Kelman, D., & Rafe, J. (2011). *Mythological translations: Drama, poetry and the language of myth*. Retrieved from https://www.intellectbooks.com/asset/857/atr-12.1-kelman.pdf

Kuritz, P. (1988). *The making of theatre history* (1st ed.). Los Angeles, CA: Prentice Hall College.

Lane, Y. (1960). *The psychology of the actor*. New York: The John Day Company.

Meyer-Dinkgrafe, D. (2001). *Approaches to acting: Past and present*. London: Continuum.

Miall, D. S., & Kuiken, D. (1994). Foregrounding, defamiliarization, and affect: Response to literary stories. *Poetics, 22*, 389–407.

Moore, S. (1965). *The Stanislavski system: The professional training of an actor*. New York: Penguin Handbooks.

Pafumi, H. (2012). Why I am a theatre artist. *theatreWashington*. Retrieved from http://theatrewashington.org/content/why-i-am-theatre-artist

Pearsall, J., & Hanks, P. (Eds.). (2010). *Oxford dictionary of English* (3rd ed.). Oxford: Oxford University Press.

Rayfield, D. (1998). *Anton Chekhov: A life*. London: Northwestern University Press.

Sawoski, P. (2012). *The Stanislavski system: Growth and methodology*. Second Edition Paper. Retrieved from homepage.smc.edu/sawoski_perviz/Stanislavski.pdf

Shevtsova, M. (2002). Appropriating Pierre Bourdieu's champ and habitus for sociology of stage productions. *Contemporary Theatre Review, 12*(3), 35–66.

Stanislavski, C. (1937). *An actor prepares* (E. R. Hapgood, Trans., 8th ed.). London: Lowe & Brydone.

Stanislavski, C. (1958). *Stanislavski's legacy*. New York: Theatre Art Books.

Stanislavski, C. (1962). *Stanislavsky my life in art* (J. J. Robbins, Trans.). New York: Geoffrey Bles, Ltd.

2 Seeking identity: searching for self

> There is much uncertainty in my mind about the meaning of "Self". For me self, which is not the ego, is the person who is me, who is only me, who has totality based on the operation of the maturational process. At the same time the self has parts, and in fact is constituted of these parts.
>
> (Winnicott, 1989, p. 271)

Identifying identity

Professor Martin Sökefeld (1999) explained how the concept of "identity"' has undergone a paradigmatic shift in recent decades. From a Western anthropological position, Sökefeld said that in the past, identity's meaning was "sameness", whereas in psychology, that sameness meant "selfsameness". Sameness, in this context, refers to the self in relation to others. This ideology of sameness was accepted by psychologists such as Erik Erikson (1980), who thought defining self-identity in relation to the individual's environment is a healthy approach. Erikson wrote, "The term 'identity' expresses such a mutual relation in that it connotes both a persistent sameness within oneself (selfsameness) and a persistent sharing of some kind of essential characteristics with others" (p. 109). The group identity of others, therefore, affects the individual's sense of identity, and as a psychologist who believed in *identities*, Erikson considered this relationship between the two a healthy approach.

Sökefeld (1999) continued to deliberate that, for anthropologists, identity, which was typically used in the context of ethnic identity, was understood as a "disposition of basic personality features acquired mostly during childhood and, once integrated, were more or less fixed. This identity made a human being a person and an acting individual" (p. 417). Following this train of thought, one can say that identity was seen as a building block, if you like, that helped construct the self. This understanding follows the common Western notion that identity is "the fact/characteristics of being who or what a person or thing is" (Pearsall & Hanks, 2010). However, ask any group of individuals for their definition of identity and, without a doubt, you will receive numerous responses that depend on their positionality. Identity is a complex concept that encompasses such factors as personality, gender, upbringing, education, opinions, DNA, desire, wants, needs, religion, language, traditions, heritage, culture, occupation and emotions.

As an individual with a complex cultural heritage, I consider my identity to be separated into two parts: my individual identity (or the multifaceted aspects that constitute my personality and behaviour) and my ethnic identity (the cultural make-up that is Persian-Armenian-Australian). The author of *The Promise of Potential*, Jodi Davis (2007), said that "all people have an identity defined by their cultural classifications (nationality, race, religion and gender) as well as by societal characterizations (family, career, and position or title)" (p. 7). Davis suggested that identity is every characteristic that helps to construct who we are as human beings and that this whole is divided up into two significant parts: our "internal identity" and our "external identity" (p. 7). Through her illustrations, she made a clear distinction between the characteristics that determine one's internal identity and those that determine external identity, thus allowing us to examine the complexion of the societal characterisations and the cultural classifications that construct the self. Davis (2007) suggested that "internal identity" is formed by our personal truths, what and who we are in our deepest core, whereas "external identity" occurs via characteristics that are bestowed upon us through other people or society – that is, our environment. She further stated that our identity is formed in direct relation to the concentric circles in our lives or "Relationship Circles of Influence" (p. 10), beginning in early childhood when we first start to discover the self, and it continues to develop and change all the way through adolescence and adulthood.

As far back as is documented, the concepts of self and identity have gone hand in hand. Researchers have long considered the self as both a product of situations and a shaper of behaviour in certain situations in that "self and identity are predicted to influence what people are motivated to do, how they think and make sense of themselves and others, the actions they take, and their feelings and ability to control or regulate themselves" (Oyserman, Elmore, & Smith, 2012, p. 70). Predating Davis, paediatrician and psychoanalyst Donald Winnicott (1965) acknowledged that self is very much linked to our behaviour and thus embodies our emotions and reactions, as well as the way we act in the world. He believed that every individual has a "true self" (private) and a "false self" (public). Winnicott determined that philosophical and psychoanalytic ideas about the *self* can be very complex and thus adapted the terminology of the founding father of psychoanalysis, Sigmund Freud (Freud & Strachey, 1991), of the Id and the Ego to describe different functions of a person's psychology. In its most humble terms, the Id is the primitive and unorganised component of an individual's psyche, and the Ego is the organised part. Freud considered the Id to be present from birth and that it holds the inherent qualities of a person, such as biological personality traits, sexual desires, impulses, needs and wants, whereas the Ego develops post birth to act as the intellectual-cognitive decision maker or mediator between the unrealistic instinctual drives of the Id and the external necessities of the real world (as cited in Storr, 1989). For Winnicott, the Id is, therefore, the true self and the Ego is the false self. This was important, as Winnicott (1965) thought only the true self is real and can be fully creative in contrast to the false self that is polite, well mannered and compliant to other people's expectations of how the individual should, in fact, behave. Further, both Winnicott and Davis proposed that identity and self

26 Seeking identity

are very much interrelated within our social environments. Winnicott (1965) used the terms "healthy and unhealthy environment", whereas Davis (2007) defined it as our "circles of influence".

I imagine that everyone acts differently around different groups of people. The mask we wear differs depending on whether we are at work, with our spouse, with our children, with our friends or particular groups of friends or alone with our own thoughts within our private space. All of these aspects make up who we are as whole persons; however, as an Armenian, I have other elucidations that are based within my cultural understandings and the way that I was raised. These understandings not only helped form my sense of identity but also influenced the way in which I exist, function and observe others and myself within the world. While I may not have used the specific definitions that Davis (2007) and Winnicott (1965) employed in their understandings of self, I have often probed the puzzle of whether individuals forge their own path in the world or whether that path is predestined. This conundrum or collision of my Western culture and Eastern culture has come to have significance when I ponder whether my decision in choosing the theatre as a vocation was a result of nature or nurture, with nature being my ճակատագիր (that which was inherited or genetically predetermined by my Armenian cultural heritage) and nurture referring to the predominantly Western environmental and educational influences and experiences imposed upon me after birth. In shadowing Winnicott's and Davis's suggestions regarding the interrelations between identity, self and social environment, it is also important to recognise that these environments are ever changing. This complex idea of evolution may be better understood through philosopher Gilles Deleuze's notion of *becoming* (Biehl & Locke, 2010).

Becoming, according to Deleuze, refers to an individual's susceptibility to being indefinitely open to new relationships, new friendships and new paths and not habituated to fixed ideas or ways of thinking. Deleuze's most critical philosophical differences were between the idea of the process of becoming and that of history. He was never against history, but he did consider that history is a form of documentation and therefore on the side of necessity and capture only, whereas becoming is on the side of contingency and creation (as cited in Lundy, 2012). Alongside fellow French theorist Félix Guattari, Deleuze questioned extensively the philosophy of history itself, believing that history is much more than an attempt to represent the past as it *actually* happened. Deleuze considered that to understand history truly, one needs to return to the *conditions* of the events themselves, not only how the event arose and caused another event and so forth (as cited in Bell & Colebrook, 2009). Deleuze (1995) wrote, "Becoming is not a part of history. History amounts only to the set of preconditions, however recent, that one leaves behind in order to 'become' that is, to create something new" (p. 171). While there are many interpretations and understandings of Deleuze's philosophy of becoming as a theoretical framework, when understood in relation to an individual's agency, it is quite liberating, as it suggests that an individual's identity is not bound by history or predetermined by specific circumstances. Rather, individuals have the ability, agency or, almost, imperative to keep changing the course of their identities and circumstances. At first glance, Deleuze's notion of *becoming* may seem to contradict the Armenian concept of Ճակատագիր. However, I do not believe that it does; rather, it is a paradox. It is important to remember that Ճակատագիր does not mean one never strives to evolve into anything because "whatever will be will be". Instead, Ճակատագիր suggests that a person is constantly evolving and becoming a certain individual, potentially steered by another innate (transcendent) guiding element. In *The Paradox of Becoming*, Geoffrey DeGraff (2008) explained this paradox wonderfully:

> We live in the same world, but in different worlds. The differences come partly from our living in different places. If you live to the east of a mountain and I to the west, my world will have a mountain blocking its sunrises, and yours its sunsets. . . . Our worlds are also different in the sense that each person can move from one world to another – sometimes very quickly – over time.
>
> (p. 7)

Recalling Sökefeld's (1999) earlier suggestions of "selfsameness" and adopting a Deleuzian understanding that we are not bound by current circumstance or history but are in fact changeable, I consider identity ever evolving. We adapt and change depending on our social-cultural context and through insights encountered about ourselves. Davis (2007) would agree and say that once we have an awareness of this ability for change, we realise that we are not fixed by our external descriptors but, rather, can move forward to unlock and understand the underlying essence of our *true* identities through the acquisition of knowledge about ourselves.

In *A Stirring Alphabet of Thought*, Marcelo Svirsky (2009) appreciated this Deleuzian philosophy and agreed that everything is in a "state of becoming". He asserted that "becoming is a transfer of forces and a pre-philosophical condition of a thought of immanence. It is a process of transformation of intensities, and takes place in a zone of the indiscernible" (p. 322). While Deleuze's (1995) ideas were primarily political, they can justly be transposed into the theatrical world when examining the motivations that can influence a director's pursuit of identity. One can say that individuals who choose the path of director, to some extent, are toying with this *state of becoming* by pursuing a creative leadership role in order to find their unique persona within the establishment of theatre and yet never arriving. For instance, for directors, artistic considerations mixed with personal aspirations drive the need to *become* more skilled and effective with every show they direct. They may aspire to be braver with their choices and expose more of their own beliefs through the characters within the play and the story, or they may simply desire to attract larger audiences and, in doing so, receive higher praise from their peers and the public. In this research, particularly, I found these two ideas of "becoming as identity" and "becoming as a more proficient director" to be intrinsically linked as I probed deeper into the role of the directors and the possible motivations of the individual who pursues a path into the profession.

Philosopher Georg Wilhelm Hegel (2003) also considered self to be relative and conditional to the subject's historical and relational environment. Self is not fixed but rather fluid and subject to a person's setting and situation at the time. Further,

28 Seeking identity

Hegel suggested that we as individuals are all separate from one another, yet within those separations, we are proportional to the other subjects around us. This is comparable to Davis's (2007) internal versus external influences. Michael Inwood (2002) described Hegel's notion of self using Hegel's analogy of the billiard ball in relation to force. Inwood articulated that, similar to a billiard ball, we are separate entities until we come into contact with another billiard ball in that "the effect that an impact that x has on an object y depends on the nature of y as well as on that of x" (p. 439). Although the billiard ball itself does not change, the effect that the external environment and the influences the other balls have on it will determine the way it reacts. Similarly, as individuals, we are highly influenced by causal invasions via external means; thus, self and our struggle for self-recognition and conciseness does not stay fixed but is relative to each setting. For Hegel, this essence of self is akin to searching for what is behind appearance, like "peeling the layers off the onion" (as cited in Blunden, 2010, p. 61). Hegel did not believe that there is an absolute end point to this process. Instead, he viewed *essence* as a continual process of probing into one's self and bringing to light what is behind it, and this evolution never concludes (as cited in Blunden, 2010). This notion of self, as Hegel understood it, supports Davis's (2007) and Deleuze's (as cited in Biehl, J. & Locke, P., 2010) ideas that we as individuals are always in a state of becoming, and this is contingent on our environment at the time.

Within this formation of identity also lies an interesting concept called "identity crisis" (Erikson, 1968). This odd notion may sound dramatic in nature, yet the concept has frequently been used by philosophers such as Hegel and by psychologists in contemporary times. The origin of the term "identity crisis" is commonly attributed to the work of Erikson (1963, 1968), who began to investigate loss of identity in the developing stages of adolescence as the most important struggle individuals face during their lives. Erikson commented that although the quotation marks that bracket "identity crisis" made it sound dramatic, the term is not as fatal as that. Instead, "identity crisis" is a suggestive term that arouses a mixture of thoughts and feelings, such as curiosity, mirth and discomfort, and while it is not calamitous, for an individual, it is a necessary turning point and a crucial moment when development needs to move one way or another, "marshalling resources of growth, recovery, and further differentiation" (Erikson, 1968, p. 16). Duane Schultz and Sydney Schultz (2008) followed on from Erikson's (1963) work and stated that identity is connected with the Ego, and between the ages of 12 and 18, we as individuals embark on a crucial stage of development in which we begin to shape our core identities. It is at this stage that we form our self-image, assimilating our ideas about ourselves and ideas about what others think of us. It is essential to note here that, fundamentally, the concept of the Ego (as was initiated by Freud [Freud & Strachey, 1991]) suggests that most of an individual's development (if not all) is done by the age of 5. Erikson and his predecessors, however, believed that the development of the Ego is an ongoing process, and although the majority of it predominantly happens in childhood and adolescence, it does not end at a certain age but is in fact fluid.

Schultz and Schultz (2008) asserted that "adolescents begin to experiment with different roles and ideologies, trying to determine the most compatible fit" (p. 168). Failure to do this results in an identity crisis in which individuals not only seem not to know who they are or what they are but more importantly, they fail to recognise where they belong and where they aspire to go (Schultz & Schultz, 2008). Erikson (1963) and Schultz and Schultz (2008) discussed that this specific period of crisis in which individuals pursue a lengthy exploration into the different ways they can be viewed within the world occurs at every stage but at different levels of intensity and importance. Erikson (1963) outlined that all the various stages of "crisis" were important to the individual's construction of identity and, in his theory of psychosocial development, suggested these stages came in eight distinct parts, which he called the "eight ages of man".

In *Childhood and Society*, Erikson (1963) outlined the significance of these eight ages and emphasised that in order for individuals to have a healthy personality, they must successfully complete, construct and resolve all eight stages. Failing to do so leads to a loss of identity and a further sense of crisis down the line. Comparably, if I consider Erikson's reasons behind loss of identity alongside Hegel's (2003) notions of self, then it seems as though construction plays a vital role within the development of one's sense of self. However, it is critical to acknowledge that Hegel and Erikson had contrasting views on how the self is formed. Hegel perceived character and personality as developing relative to the individual's historical circumstance, whereas Erikson believed it develops in a predetermined order. Hegel saw the self as a separate entity and Erikson saw it as relational to the other ages (stages) that had come before. Nonetheless, both reflected upon the abrupt interruptions within a person's progression of self that causes this loss of identity. Erikson (1963) considered that every age has a mini crisis, but the main "identity crisis" occurs during the adolescent period when development is interrupted or incomplete. In contrast, for Hegel (2003), "identity crisis" transpires when individuals are forced into a different situation that interrupts their construction of their preconditioned self according to their past circumstances. Either way, the concept of "identity crisis" is fascinating, and in Chapter 4, "Dating Directing: Finding the Perfect Match", I raise it again as I reflect upon my experiences and those of other directors who have encountered this loss of identity. In doing so, I examine the various facets of my ipseity to try to determine if such awareness assisted me in learning and relearning aspects of my *beingness* in relation to the practices of directing. For instance, did my pursuit of self via these interruptions enable me to find a sense of identity as a director or did, in fact, directing assist in the identity formation?

These discussions on internal and external identity or the true self versus the false self resound with ideas about the private and public façades (or masks) that are often raised within performing arts contexts – the sort of double-negative process that exists between actor and character, so to speak (Archer, 1888; Schechner, 1985). However, my allusion to these façades refers not so much to the "character" that the actor aspires to encapsulate but rather to the actor her/himself, whose identity is divided into this sense of the private self and public self. That is to say, the way they "act", for example, with awareness of an audience differs from how they present themselves if they are alone, rehearsing or performing within their own private setting. This attentiveness to the private and public initiated from the work of theatre luminary Stanislavski (1937) as he began to develop an acting method that helps actors to appear more naturalistic or realistic on stage. Stanislavski (1937) developed the exercise called the "Public Solitude", which attempts to give the actor the skill and conviction to be caught up in a moment of solitude as the character yet still be in a public setting.

Since Stanislavski's time, many other performing arts practitioners have further developed these ideas, such as acting teacher-director Lee Strasberg, who created the acting exercise called the "Private Moment" (Strasberg & Schechner, 1964), which moves away from the character and brings the focus back to the actor. Strasberg's interpretation is more in line with my inclination towards the idea of the private and public façade, as he challenged actors to be engrossed in an activity within their own private rooms or settings, unaware or undeterred by external audiences gazing in, thus encouraging actors to reveal their true selves within the role. For these theatre practitioners, the private self is revealed when actors are able to explore the true nature of privacy in front of the audience without allowing the audience to affect their performance. The public self emerges when actors are aware of the audience's observation and, therefore, manipulate their behaviour to portray a non-truthful representation. Of course, any deliberations between the private and public selves within the context of the performing arts are full of complexities and contradictions, as explored by numerous performance theorists.

Richard Schechner (1985), Denis Diderot (1883) and William Archer (1888) were intellectual thinkers who, in their own identifiable ways, discussed the paradox of the actor's identity. Schechner (1985), in particular, described the actor's identity in performance as combining the "not me" and the "not not me" (p. 112), demonstrating that, in fact, by the actor taking on another self that is the *character*, the question of whether the actor can ever be the true self in a performative setting becomes somewhat erroneous when theatre itself is an un-real setting. Again, although this thread of discussion is detached from the field of psychology, I find it fascinating how such identifications as *private* and *public* trail into other areas of employment and, specifically for this research, into the theatre.

There are abundant systems or formulas to rationalise our understandings of identity (or rather identities), and in applying these concepts, it is imperative to remember that they are multifaceted and subjectively debated depending on positionality. Likewise, who we are and how our identities and personalities are formed are also dependent on our particular environments, identifications and cultural influences, which in my case are inherent of Eastern and Western beliefs. Having said that, I do consider that, fundamentally, certain key factors, such as those proposed by Davis (2007), Winnicott (1965) and Erikson (1963, 1968, 1980), continue to affect the course of a journey of self-discovery into the multiple facets of one's ipseity.

What's in a home?

Similar to identity and self, the concept of home can mean so many things to different individuals. In a common-sense daily understanding, home is defined as "one's place of residence" or "the social unit formed by a family living together" (Pearsall &

Hanks, 2010). Growing up, I found it difficult to adhere to English maxims such as *home is where the heart is* and *there's no place like home* since neither seemed to fit my situation. For me, home was a mere building where I ate and slept, but the building itself had no emotional value. I was constantly envious of friends (and still am) who still had the homes in which they had grown up, with childhood bedrooms left unchanged and personal engravings on the wall, which held so many memories of long dinner-table conversations and hiding places where numerous games were played. Over time, as I moved out of my childhood home and created my private places of dwelling, the idea of home shifted from a place of residence into a more metaphorical consciousness of the word. Home evolved to become more than just a place with locational coordinates and instead became a space that I alone created.

Nonetheless, this understanding of "home" can differ depending on each individual's cultural background. For example, in Armenian, the word used is տուն, which simply means "house" or "where one lives" (Ourishian, 2014); in German, from which the English word originates, the word is *heim*, meaning "home"; in Lithuanian, it is *šeima*, meaning "family"; and the Greek derivative is *kitzein*, meaning "to inhabit" (Pearsall & Hanks, 2010). Therefore, to identify the word in one manner only is erroneous, as every school of thought and every culture has a different understanding of and relationship with the concept. Lucille Korwin-Kossakowski (2013) agreed that "home" can mean several things depending on the individual; however, she added that, while this may be the case, "the lack of one [home] can create a universal feeling of displacement and dislocation" (p. 6). Susan Friedman (2004) asked, "Is home a place? A memory? An ideal? An imagined space? The black hole of desire?" (p. 195). This idea of home and its indeterminacy has constantly plagued me. Although the idea of home for me suggests a stable place, Janet Zandy (1990), along with author and activist bell hooks (1990), observed that home is an idea that can, at times, simply be a place of memory. Memory in itself is a complex notion, which Zandy, hooks and novelist-essayist Salman Rushdie (1992) often talked about in connection with displacement, belonging and the individual's need for that illusory sense of home. In regard to my familiarities with home and memory, I related to them as "the complex relation of personal experiences, the shared histories or communities and their modes of transmission" (Besser, Baronian, & Jansen, 2006, p. 11). Therefore, my longing for home seemed to be on two levels: the memory of my "real" home, which I shared with my parents in Australia and which held my personal experiences, and my imagined and illusionary sense of home – my homeland of Armenia, which held the cultural histories of my community. While this research focuses on "home" from the individual's perspective as a place of dwelling, acceptance and belonging, I am aware that home is a problematic and charged term and has been for years. For example, home and belonging are what the Israelis and the Palestinians are persistently fighting over. However, for the purposes of this study, while I cannot deny the political undercurrents of home on a global scale, or what it means to various cultures, the political connotations were beyond the scope of this research. This understanding proved stimulating, as throughout the scholarship, I found myself discussing the changeability of my awareness of my ideas of

32 Seeking identity

home: from the imaginary idea of what belonging and acceptance would be like in Armenia, for example, to the contradictory reality of what actually occurred.

However, my philosophies of home prove even more interesting when examined alongside my cultural position as an Armenian, for by circumstance, Armenians are a people of displacement and unhoming. In *The Armenians: Past and Present in the Making of National Identity*, Edmund Herzig and Marina Kurkchiyan (2004) discussed extensively the historical forces and current social and political developments that shaped who the Armenian people are today and why for over 1,700 years they have been a civilisation plagued by diaspora. Susan Pattie (1999) wrote that, for Armenians, this diaspora is not only a result of the 1915 Armenian Genocide but also that for many centuries, the Armenian world has been constructed of interconnected communities without a governing body of their own. Pattie stated that although the vast majority of people have remained on the territory of their ancestors in Armenia, because of historical and political circumstances, parts of the land are now known as Eastern Turkey and the Caucasus. The geographical constructs that Pattie discussed become pivotal as they in themselves cause qualities of displacement and unbelonging that contribute towards the individual's overall loss of identity or sense of place within the world.

As I studied the widespread literature available on diaspora, I found that the relationship between home and identity was a common motif. Sujata Ramachandran (2013) reported on this correlation, and in her article, she seemed to be asking all the questions on which I had been endlessly deliberating. Ramachandran asked,

> What constitutes "home" for the diaspora? Is "home" a place where the diaspora was born or originates from? Is "home" the place where one's parents or grandparents were born? Is it where one now lives? Does it mean one's country of birth or residence? Or does it signify the locality or region one came from? Is it a physical space, a geographical space synonymous with the boundaries of the nation-state? Or an imaginary, symbolic space shaped by personal experiences and close relationships within the diaspora? Do diasporans have one home they identify with, two homes (based on birth and settlement) or multiple homes imbued with different meanings? Equally important, what are the effects on diaspora local and transnational engagement of identifications with these real and imagined spaces?
>
> (para. 2)

Ramachandran's inquiries are pivotal to the central themes that I explored and raised constantly throughout this work, particularly in Chapter 3, "Affinity with Armenia: A Narrative in Two Parts", where I directly question my ideas of Armenia as an imagined homeland that I was longing to see and belong to. In Chapter 4, "Dating Directing: Finding the Perfect Match", I also ask whether my identity is a product of my country of birth or residence or whether it signifies my heritage. That is, am I more Persian (Armenian), Australian (Armenian) or Armenian (Armenian)?

It can be supposed that Armenians' sensitivity towards home depends on their own pursuit of *becoming*. Pattie (1999) deliberated on these links between identity

Seeking identity

and homeland and said, "For an Armenian this tangled mass of approaches to the question of ethnic identity and diaspora/homeland relations is highly appropriate" (p. 3). However, I imagine that, to some extent, the distress of not being in one's homeland or the possibility of once again being forced away has a subliminal effect on one's search for identity, as it did with me. When people have been involuntarily pushed off their ancestral land or reside on a land that is theirs by right but not by law, then the question of who they are and what their identity is will be inevitable. Therefore, they begin to feel like wanderers travelling back and forth in a constant search for a home. However, as I did with identity, I wonder if I can challenge my understanding of home as a fixed place of dwelling so that it can evolve to mean something else. Pattie (1999) believes this is possible, as she argued, "Like identity itself, the concepts of Return, homeland, and diaspora are all continually in the process of construction. They interact with each other and other factors both within the Armenian world and the varied contexts within which Armenians live" (p. 3). While this English understanding of home is, in essence, to feel or be at home or to feel comfortable and relaxed, like me, several scholars, such as those formerly mentioned, have continually interrogated the meaning of home.

As I approached my mid-thirties, my association with home was once again changed significantly. Suddenly, a longing for a deeper connection to an established place had taken effect, and I found myself often becoming homesick, but homesick for where I did not know. Friedman (2004) believes that homesickness is experienced viscerally and that longing for home is not the mind's but the body's desire and "home comes into being most powerfully when it is gone, lost, left behind, desired and imagined" (p. 202). It seems that this impression is not too far removed from the Armenian proverb Երբ վոր դու հեռանաս կո սեփական տունիչ, հետու կիմանաս դրա արժէքը, որդեվ մենակ կրլինես (*When you are far away from home, then you will know its value because you will be alone*). Brett Kaplan (2007) considered this "longing" as not an uncommon event for a displaced individual with a heritage of diaspora, as eventually home becomes "a mode of interpretative in-betweenness" (p. 91), hence my association of home with the wanderer. Regrettably, though, I was beginning to recognise that my utopian desire for a home may well have been a goal that could only be attained (or imagined) in states of loss.

Belonging and displacement

Concepts of home, belonging and displacement are concurrent for an individual of the diaspora. The need for a fixed home or a return to a (imaginary) homeland, although directly linked to belonging and displacement, presents varying qualities. Immigrants commonly experience notions of belonging, unhoming, displacement, the *in-between* and the *other* as working conjointly. Gregory Walton (2007) discussed these matters and, in reference to belonging, said that its significance lies in the fact that it is a primal need, arguing that a sense of belonging is fundamental to human happiness and well-being, and he linked all the aspects of who and how we are in relationship to this embryonic "need to belong". It is not surprising, then, that for individuals who have struggled with identity in ethnic contexts and who regularly feel stuck between two (or more) cultures, belonging is an aspect of their identities that they habitually have difficulty accessing.

Critical theorist Homi Bhabha (1992) understood that "for many immigrants, any sense of belonging becomes close to impossible (or very difficult) to attain as a result of the 'unhomely' spaces that surround them" (as cited in Golparian, 2012, p. 21). The "unhomely", as understood through Bhabha, is not a state of lacking a home, as the word might suggest, but is the creeping recognition that the line between the world and the home is becoming disorientated and breaking down. He stated, "In that displacement the border between home and world becomes confused; and, uncannily, the private and the public become part of each other, forcing upon us a vision that is as divided as it is disorienting" (Bhabha, 1992, p. 141). The question of belonging and unhoming are aspects of my identity with which I have struggled, like so many of my contemporaries.

In *Belonging: A Culture of Place*, hooks (2009) chronicled her own struggles as she likewise attempted to find her position in the world. She moved from place to place to find where it was she belonged, only to end up at the beginning again. hooks wrote, "talking about place, where we belong is a constant subject for many of us. Many folks have no sense of place and therefore feel an impending doom" (2009, p. 2). Although hooks is not a theatre practitioner, I do find it comforting to know that the exploration of this issue seems to be common for individuals who have been displaced, whether through migration or, as with hooks, through racial discrimination. Like hooks, I believe that "to fully belong anywhere, one must understand the ground of one's own being" (2009, p. 2), which prompts another Armenian saying: Շէտե ուզում ես իմանաս թէ որտեղ ես գնում, հէտ նայիր թէ որտեղ ես եէ (*If you want to know to where you are going, then look to where you have been*).

While belonging and displacement both signify a loss of a place, it is important not to associate the terms only with the experiences of those people of the diaspora. Displacement, for instance, is likely to befall anyone and not only those who have been forcibly moved from their homelands. Artist and researcher Shaya Golparian (2012) suggested that displacement is not about absence of a place or home at all but, more importantly, concerned with a loss of context that is physically and temporally situated in history and culture. She said, "It is exactly the loss of that positioning, both in the physical and the non-physical sense, that creates a sense of displacement" (p. 44). Therefore, my experiences of cultural displacement are also comparable to Golparian's suggestions of circumstance as a motivation for trying to find a place of contentment to be connected with/in, whether that connection be physical or spiritual or both. It is also important to recognise that, as I discuss displacement, I do not suggest in any way that the forced or felt dislocation of identity is exclusive to those with mixed cultural backgrounds; however, for the purposes of my research, I will largely refer to displacement in direct correlation to those who have been or are *culturally displaced*.

Although belonging and displacement are two detached terms, in my mind, they represent the same concept of *not fitting in*. Therefore, the struggles against these feelings of displacement go conjointly with my sense of unhoming and the *in-between* in combination with that deep desire to belong or to assimilate. When belonging is not achieved, displacement arises.

Flirting with the "unhomely" and the "in-between"

My familiarities with displacement resonated with Bhabha's (1992) concept of the "unhomely". The term the "unhomely" may seem strange, but Bhabha, conceding that it is awkward, asked that we permit him this "awkward word" (p. 141). He wrote,

> To be unhomed is not to be homeless, nor can the "unhomely" be easily accommodated in that familiar division of social life into private and the public's spheres. The unhomely moment creeps upon you stealthily as your own shadow and suddenly you find yourself taking the measure of your dwelling in a state of "incredulous terror". And it is at this point that the world first shrinks and then expands enormously.
>
> (p. 141)

Bhabha's ideas of the unhomely feel familiar to me. There have been several occasions in my life when my ideas of *home* or position within a certain situation have become disorientated, and as a result, following Bhabha (1992), I have felt *unhomed*. Comparable to being displaced, in my moments of unhoming, the borders between my worlds become confused when, for example, what I had come to know and recognise was interrupted by the reality of the situation as instigated by someone or something else. I will discuss several of these moments within this exegesis; however, the first one I clearly recall was when I was 13 years old and received my first passport. To some extent, I consider this a pivotal juncture in my life in which I not only began consciously to question my sense of identity and where I belonged but also began to feel displaced.

Even as an adolescent, I knew what a special occasion it was to receive a passport, and I could not wait until I held that document in my hands. However, once I opened it up, my unhoming and sense of displacement unexpectedly began. Immediately, I noticed that under nationality it read "Australian".

I turned to my father and said, "Dad, they've made a mistake. I'm not Australian; I'm Armenian".

"Yes", my father cautiously replied, "you are right; your nationality is Armenian, but officially you're nationalised as an Australian".

I was so confused. Bhabha (1992) explained that an "unhomely moment relates to the traumatic ambivalences of a personal, psychic history to the wider disjunctions of political existence" (p. 174). It was obvious to me that, as Bhabha had observed, my confusion lay in the dislocation of my personal situation and the complicated legalities of the socio-political contexts concerning official identification. Here my heart was telling me one thing, and the Australian government was telling me another.

Being situated in a liminal space, although difficult, is not an uncommon position for people caught in situations of mixed affiliations. Many scholars, such as Bhabha (1992), Golparian (2012) and Rushdie (1992), who have themselves

36 Seeking identity

experienced immigration, have identified with this liminal space of being stuck between two (or more) cultures. In fact, writer and philosopher Frantz Fanon (1986) commented on how cultural identities are among the few privileged societies to explore this unique threshold. Literary theorist and intellectual Edward Said (1998) repeatedly spoke about this state of "in-between" and the struggle of belonging to two or more worlds, which often results in a feeling of alienation from both. Said (1998) described his own self-perception as a state of divided allegiance. Bhabha (1994) likewise believed that the space of "in-between" was a tussle of wanting to belong and not belonging at the same time, which immigrants repeatedly experience.

Golparian (2012) declared that, as a "Persian, Quebecois and Canadian, Francophone and Anglophone, emigrant and immigrant" (p. 3), there is no other place with which she can identify but the *in-between*. Echoing Bhabha's (1994) thoughts, she described the in-between as "an ambiguous and shifting ground where immigrants often find themselves as simultaneously insiders and outsiders to two (or more) cultures. In-between, can be a very troubling space for an immigrant to have to negotiate her identity" (Golparian, 2012, p. 47). While these scholars have their own unique ways of articulating the *in-between* space, surprisingly, they all appear to transform its identification from what seems at first to be a negative space into a source of pride – a distinctive state, if you like – where new signs of identity are forged and a rebirth takes effect. The "in-between spaces provide the terrain[s] for elaborating strategies of selfhood – singular or communal – that initiate new signs of identity, and innovative sites of collaboration" (Bhabha, 1994, pp. 1–2). Bhabha took what may appear at first to be a defect or an indeterminate identity and celebrated difference as a cultural marker and indeterminacy as a signifier of a new identity. Although initially being situated *in-between* may have been an undesirable position, as Bhabha suggested, it forced me to initiate a new sense of who I am and, therefore, a new sense of my identity was formed.

My state of *in-betweenness* is a tension between three worlds. However, I refuse to identify with being a Persian, as I am an Armenian Christian whose family deliberately left Iran after the 1979 Islamic Revolution, which brought about the persecution of non-Muslim ethnicities. Second, while culturally, traditionally and linguistically I was brought up as an Armenian, I was not born there, nor do I have any immediate forebears who were settlers from the region. Third, while I am legally nationalised as an Australian, often I do not recognise myself as one because of my ethnicity. Rushdie (1992) proposed that migrants feel as though they are straddling two (or more) cultures, adding that it is precisely in this space between cultures that an individual has the capacity to transfer out of one or the other to develop a unique personal identity. While I was considering the concepts of the *unhomely* and the *in-between*, additional thoughts emerged. I recalled memories I had of being *unhomed* and the various other happenings that centred on my nationality, and I recognised that my memories were fundamentally a consequence of something far more significant. In each situation that I encountered, I was in the position of the *other*, and I was being displaced – whether during a passport misidentification, being bullied as an adolescent because of my ethnic *non-Anglo-Saxon* appearance, being interrogated as an adult at a Los Angeles airport for being an Iranian or, finally, being staunchly rejected by native Armenians for being too Australian. In whichever way the criticisms were constructed, my experiences were littered with an underlying element of being *othered*, which ultimately caused my sense of displacement. I wondered, if I accepted that memory by its very nature is a process of displacement in itself (Besser et al., 2006), then could the current sense of *unhoming* be fundamentally linked to my experiences of *othering*?

The other

According to Bhabha (1983), the *other* refers to the absorption of stereotypical assumptions as an ideological operation. Once stereotyped individuals are placed into a group and do not perform or conform to the stereotypical assumptions made against them, they are immediately seen as being the *other*.

As a young adult, I made jokes about my ethnicity before anyone else did. I called myself a wog[1] and made fun of my *ethnicisms* – I still do. Now, reflecting on those moments, I cannot help but question whether my admissions of *imperfection* (according to Australians' perception of perfection) made the self-mocking acceptable or was it simply a method of self-protection so that others did not *other* me first and, in turn, contribute to my *own unhoming*? Michael Pickering (2001) suggested that "*othering* operates as a strategy of symbolic exclusion which makes it easier for people to blame *the other* for their society's problems" (p. 48). I recall several occasions when I was asked what my nationality was. I would reply "Australian", with the hope of being accepted. Often, this answer raised a smirk and was countered with, "Oh yes, but what is your background?", immediately rejecting the possibility that being an Australian might actually *be* my only background. Of course, I knew what they were referring to. It was their idea of the stereotype of the Australian – that tall-tanned-fit-blonde-haired woman who loves to surf and lives near the beach. When I was younger, this predicament frequently bothered me, but over time, I arrived at the realisation that, although being caught somewhere in-between was not ideal, on occasion, it did serve as an advantage.

In Europe, I often encountered people who associated Australians with convicts, and although they made a joke of it, I[2] could tell that deep down they considered Australians uncultured. Immediately, it reminded me of the *cultural cringe* (Hume, 1991). While the cultural cringe goes beyond the scope of this study, it is a reflection on human relations that is important for me to acknowledge. It is a term coined by Arthur Angell Phillips (1950) who used the phrase to describe Australians' lack of faith in their own culture. He discussed how some intellectual Australians struggled with their feelings of cultural inferiority when it came to music, arts and theatre, for example, in comparison with the Euro-American world. What is interesting about this observation from Phillips is that I too found myself developing a sense of inferiority and humiliation when I was compared with an average Australian stereotype predetermined by "foreigners". As an Australian, I knew that *our* culture was not inferior – not by any means. Although young compared with

38 *Seeking identity*

Europe, Australia has abundant historical narratives to mark the unique identities of its citizens. Nevertheless, paradoxically, I wanted them to know that culturally I was much more than an *Aussie*. Even though I wished I had contested their views on the matter, there was an aspect of me that shamefully agreed. After repeated occurrences, I noticed that these comments were affecting my behaviour to the extent that I developed a protective device to ward against such views. I began to counter the comments by announcing that, although I lived in Australia, my nationality was Armenian and not Australian. Immediately, I felt a shield of protection come over me and felt at ease.

Journalist Leonie Lamont (2005) reported on research she conducted at Monash University in 2005 involving 50 educated multicultural women whose views were sought on Australia and the idea of the cultural cringe. Through Lamont's account of the research, it was evident that the cultural cringe was still very prominent in contemporary Australia. In fact, a Middle Eastern woman who was interviewed as part of the study, when asked her opinion on Australia's culture (or lack thereof), replied, "What is there? There's barbecues, the outback. I seriously don't see what there is. When I look at my history, I think, oh my God, look where we were. You feel so proud" (para. 4). After reading several similar comments in Lamont's article, I felt relieved to know that I was not alone in my opinions on this matter. Consequently, through such observations, my behaviour also revealed a duality or double standard regarding the processes of *othering*. At the time, I despised others *othering* me but saw no harm when I *othered* myself, or other Australians, for that matter. While the notion is complex and contradictory, *othering* and *unhoming* both force the individual into an outsider's position, leaving them susceptible to the liminal space of the *in-between*. I wondered then, was *othering* something to which I subjected myself instinctively as a means of survival to protect the integrity of my identity? Or was it singularly done to me by other people's perception of what they saw as the "acceptable norm"? Either way, it was evident that whichever form these indicators take, they force immigrants into a position of exclusion, which, in essence, leads to a sense of displacement, initially through their community, and then within the wider world.

In *Stereotyping: The Politics of Representation*, Michael Pickering (2001) explored similar views and suggested that "othering helps to define the self and to affirm identity. In contrast, it divests [other individuals] of their social and cultural identities by diminishing them to their stereotyped characteristics and by casting them as silent objects" (p. 73). Pickering's use of "stereotyped characteristics" confirms that *othering* does not begin with the individual but arises through society's projection of what the *other* should be – that is, their stereotyped characteristics. Pickering's prognosis is often seen in daily Australian interaction – for example, stereotypes such as Asians cannot drive, the uneducated bogan,[3] the wog who owns a fruit shop, the blonde bimbo and the ethnic taxi driver.

Othering as a form of mockery has always been prominent in Australian culture, so much so that an Australian government website actually dedicates a section of its web content to those who would like to "get to know Australia". One of the subheadings in this section is titled "Australian Humour". This official website goes to great lengths to try to educate other societal members on what being an Aussie is all about. The Aussie humour is attributed to responses to the country's origins as a convict colony and is "dry, full of extremes, anti-authoritarian, self-mocking and ironic" (Big Black Dog Communications, 2007, para. 1). I suppose such characteristics ring true, for Australian writers and performers such as Nick Giannopoulos, Chris Lilley and Paul Fenech have built very successful careers on the backs of comedy shows that proudly promote self-mockery, as has Australian comedian Steady Eddy, who has become renowned for making fun of his own cerebral palsy. The Australian government website further indicates that, although in many cultures it is considered poor taste to find humour in difficult circumstances, such as ethnicity or disability, Australians tend to look for this lighter side and do it very effectively, as seen in our use of slang across media from sketches and series on television to films (Big Black Dog Communications, 2007).

Journalist Richard Glover (2015) noted,

> Mark Twain said Australian history was full of "the most beautiful lies" – but it's nothing compared to the lies we tell each other every day. Almost all the stereotypes about Australia – the things we actively promote and believe to be true – are the antithesis of what really goes on.
>
> (para. 1)

This self-mockery of the stereotype discussed by Glover and on the Australian government website is represented in several successful Australian television shows, such as *Acropolis Now* (Amenta et al., 1989–1992), *Wogs Out of Work* (Giannopoulos, Palomares, & Portesi, 1987), *Jonah from Tonga* (Lilley & McDonald, 2014), *Housos* (Fenech, 2011) and *Bogan Hunters* (Fenech, 2014). All mock minorities and Australia's stereotypical behaviour towards such ethnic groups. Nevertheless, I wondered, when does self-mockery of the stereotype become unfunny? During an interview session, I asked prominent Greek Australian actor and director Lex Marinos OAM his opinions on this matter or, more specifically, how marginalisation had affected his career in the performing arts. He responded, "*You know you're just put into a box, Greek, Italian, Lebanese it really doesn't matter. After a while, you just . . . you know . . . give them what they want*" (Interview, 16 August 2013). This comment resonated acutely with me, as prior to becoming a director, I too was an actor for several years and, like Marinos, I encountered the racial stereotyping.

Because I was a culturally diverse performer in Australia, my agent would call and tell me that a casting director was looking for a migrant or a foreigner. The majority of the time (if not always), I assumed the stereotype of their expectations when I walked through the door. Like Marinos, I have repeatedly found myself conforming to a predetermined stereotype of a character to secure a role. I understand that industry professionals may challenge this point of view today; however, the reality is that, although discussions about breaking down stereotypes and typecasting are pleasing, it is easy to talk about but difficult to achieve. In a society such as Australia, where a culture of self-mockery of one's background

40 *Seeking identity*

(whatever delineation that may be) is the accepted norm, it seems that the *other* cannot undergo any response but to other her/himself first through exclusion, if the person hopes to survive – survive both personally and, as Marinos and I experienced, professionally. That is, if I mock or segregate myself first, highlighting my points of difference, then it cannot be done to me, or if it is, it will not seem to have affected me as much, for I have already taken the initiative to mock my otherness. Of course, while the discomforts or embarrassments in the moment are at first lessened, the painful reverberations are not.

Said (1993) believed that no one could or should deny anyone his/her culture, whether it was long-serving traditions, habitualisation or language. In fact, he noted that prejudice perpetuates these separations and distinctiveness, stating,

> It is more rewarding – and more difficult – to think concretely and sympathetically, contrapuntally, about others than only about "us". But this also means not trying to rule others, not trying to classify them or put them in hierarchies, above all, not constantly reiterating how "our" culture or country is number one (or not number one, for that matter).
>
> (pp. 407–408)

Said's (1993) thoughts on the context of the *other* echo Bhabha's (1994) beliefs that attributes considered by society to be flaws should actually be celebrated as a cultural difference, allowing for the qualities to act as signifiers to help people forge new identities. Of course, this attitude is complicated in Australia because of the self-mocking humour. Said's specific considerations of the *other* as a positive potentiality, which should be admired instead of being denounced, may not have served me well personally when I was growing up in Australia. However, professionally, as a theatre director, the experiences that I have encountered in being the *other* have been to my advantage. These instances have led me to explore Bhabha's discussions about *third space* theory.

In an interview session conducted by Jonathan Rutherford (1990), Bhabha stated that the "third space" is an uncertain area of dialogue that develops when two or more cultures interact. Of course, I accept that Bhabha's observations were formed primarily in relation to political groups and their discourses; however, my work as a theatre director is highly dependent on this notion of the third space, which, according to Patricia Pisters (2007), Bhabha claimed was "a space of hybridity in and between cultural differences" (p. 301). Reflecting back on the discussions in Chapter 1, "Attracted to Theatre: Setting the Scene", I view the theatre as my third space, where my *otherness* and my struggles of being caught "in-between" three cultures are not seen as a hindrance but, instead, enable me to turn flaws into endless possibilities of creativity and to celebrate them as my unique qualities as a theatre maker. In this space, I personally feel that I am not the *other*, the *unhomed* or the *in-between*. Instead, I am a theatre director whose work is (for the most part) viewed as open, and while it may be veiled in political agendas and often biased, it is celebrated in a conducive, non-judgemental setting where as long as one "plays by the rules" (Bourdieu, 1977), one is allowed to express one's individuality in whichever way one pleases.

Notes

1 Officially, the term "wog" comes from the British understanding for any person who has Middle Eastern or Asian ethnicity. Unlike the United Kingdom, in Australia, this is an offensive and derogatory term, referring to any foreigner or immigrant without "white skin" (Pearsall & Hanks, 2010). Throughout this thesis, I use the term in its slang form as an ethnic or racial slur.
2 Deliberately, I stress the "I", because, honestly, I do not know if this was the truth of the situation or if it was just my reaction to the questioning.
3 The word "bogan" is a derogatory term meaning an uncouth or unsophisticated person regarded as being of low social status (Pearsall & Hanks, 2010). The term, although prominent in both Australian and New Zealand slang, for the purposes of this research, relates to the Australian "bogan", whose speech, clothing and attitude are all very specific, and project a lack of education and etiquette.

References

Amenta, P., Flanagan, K., Friedman, A., Emery, T., Smith, M., Andrikidis, P., . . . Bates, J. (Writers). (1989–1992). *Acropolis now* [Television]. C. Productions (Producer). Melbourne, Australia: Seven Network.
Archer, W. (1888). *Masks or faces? A study in the psychology of acting*. London: Longmans, Green, and Co.
Bell, J. A., & Colebrook, C. (2009). *Deleuze and history*. London: Edinburgh University Press.
Besser, S., Baronian, M. A., & Jansen, Y. (2006). Introduction: Diaspora and memory. Figures of displacement in contemporary literature, arts and politics. *Thamyris/Intersecting Place, Sex and Race, 13*, 9–16.
Bhabha, H. K. (1983). The other question, the stereotype and colonial discourse. *Oxford Journals, 24*(6), 18–36.
Bhabha, H. K. (1992). The world and the home. *Social Text, Third World and Post-Colonial Issues, 31/32*, 141–153.
Bhabha, H. K. (1994). DissemiNation: Time, narrative and the margins of the modern nation. In *The location of culture*. London: Routledge.
Biehl, J., & Locke, P. (2010). Deleuze and the anthropology of becoming. *Current Anthropology, 51*.
Big Black Dog Communications. (2007). *Australian humour*. Retrieved from http://australia.gov.au/about-australia/australian-story/austn-humour
Blunden, A. (2010). *An interdisciplinary theory of activity*. Boston, MA: BRILL.
Bourdieu, P. (1977). *An outline of a theory of practice*. Cambridge: Cambridge University Press.
Davis, J. (2007). Identity. In *The promise of potential*. Minneapolis, MN: JD Coaching and Consulting.
DeGraff, G. (2008). *The paradox of becoming*. New York, NY: Thanissaro Bhikkhu.
Deleuze, G. (1995). *Negotiations 1972–1990*. New York: Coumbia University Press.
Diderot, D. (1883). *The paradox of acting*. London: Chatto & Windus.
Erikson, E. H. (1963). *Childhood and society*. New York: W. W. Norton & Company Inc.
Erikson, E. H. (1968). *Identity: Youth and crisis*. New York: Austen Riggs Monograph.
Erikson, E. H. (1980). *Identity and the life cycle*. New York: W. W Norton & Company Inc.
Fanon, F. (1986). *Black skin white masks*. London: Pluto Press.
Fenech, P. (Writer). (2011). *Housos* [Television]. SBS (Producer). Australia.
Fenech, P. (Writer). (2014). *Bogan Hunters* [Television]. P. Fenech (Producer). Australia: SBS.

Freud, S., & Strachey, J. (1991). *On metapsychology: The theory of psychoanalysis: 'Beyond the pleasure principle,' 'the ego and the id' and other works* (A. Richards, Ed.). London: Penguin Books.

Friedman, S. S. (2004). Bodies on the move: A poetics of home and diaspora. *Tulsa Studies in Women's Literature, 23*(2), 189–212.

Giannopoulos, N., Palomares, S., & Portesi, M. (1987). *Wogs out of work* [Play]. Melbourne, Australia.

Glover, R. (2015, January 23). Let's be honest about Australia and ditch the stereotypes. *The Sydney Morning Herald*. Retrieved from www.smh.com.au/comment/lets-be-honest-about – australia-and-ditch-the-stereotypes-20150123–12txce.html

Golparian, S. (2012). *Displaced displacement: An A/r/tography performance of experinces of being unhomed*. Doctor of Philosophy, The University of British Columbia, Vancouver.

Hegel, G. W. (2003). *The phenomenology of mind* (J. B. Baillie, Trans.). New York: Dover Publications.

Herzig, E., & Kurkchiyan, M. (2004). *The Armenians: Past and present in the making of national identity*. London: Taylor & Francis.

hooks, b. (1990). *Yearning: Race, gender and cultural politics*. Boston, MA: South End Press.

hooks, b. (2009). *Belonging: A culture of place*. New York: Routledge.

Hume, L. J. (1991). Another look at the cultural cringe. *The Political Theory Newsletter*. Retrieved from https://www.cis.org.au/app/uploads/2015/07/op45.pdf

Inwood, M. (2002). *Hegel*. London: Taylor & Francis Ltd.

Kaplan, B. A. (2007). Contested, constructed home(lands): diaspora, postcolonial studies and Zionism. *Journal of Modern Jewish Studies, 6*(1), 85–100.

Korwin-Kossakowski, L. (2013). Displacement: The mandala guides me home towards different ways of knowing. *UNESCO Observatory Multi-Disciplinary Journal in the Arts, 3*(1).

Lamont, L. (2005, July 7). Now migrants adopt the cultural cringe. *Sydney Morning Herald*. Retrieved from www.smh.com.au/news/national/echoes-in-the-void/2005/07/06/1120329507214.html

Lilley, C., & McDonald, S. (Writers). (2014). *Jonah from Tonga* [Television]. C. W. Lilley & L. Waters (Producers). Melbourne, Australia: ABC.

Lundy, C. (2012). *History and becoming: Deleuze's philosophy of creativity*. London: Edinburgh University Press.

Ourishian, S. (2014). *Nayiri English-Armenian electronic dictionary*. Retrieved from Nayiri Institute www.nayiri.com/search?l=en&query=house&dt=EN_HY

Oyserman, D., Elmore, K., & Smith, G. (2012). Self, self-concept, and identity. In M. R. Leary & J. P. Tangney (Eds.), *Handbook of self and identity* (pp. 69–104). New York: The Guilford Press.

Pattie, S. P. (1999). *Longing and belonging: Issues of homeland in the Armenian diaspora*. Doctor of Philosophy, University College London, London.

Pearsall, J., & Hanks, P. (Eds.). (2010). *Oxford dictionary of English* (3rd ed.). Oxford: Oxford University Press.

Phillips, A. A. (1950). The cultural cringe. *Meanjin, 9*(4), 299–302.

Pickering, M. (2001). *Stereotyping. The politics of representation*. Basingstoke: Palgrave.

Pisters, P. (2007). Homi K. Bhabha. In F. Colman (Ed.), *Film, theory and philosophy: The key thinkers* (pp. 296–307). Montreal: McGill-Queen's University Press.

Ramachandran, S. (2013). *No place like "home": Nostalgia and attachment in diaspora engagement*. Centre for International Governance Innovation.

Rushdie, S. (1992). *Imaginary homelands, essays and criticism 1981–1991*. London: Granta Books.

Rutherford, J. (1990). The third space. Interview with Homi Bhabha. In *Identity: Community, culture, difference*. London: Lawrence and Wishart.

Said, E. W. (1993). *Culture and imperialism*. New York, NY: Vintage Books.

Said, E. W. (1998). Between worlds, Edward Said makes sense of his life. *London Review of Books, 20*(9), 3–7.

Schechner, R. (1985). *Between theater and anthropology*. Philadelphia, PA: University of Pennsylvania Press.

Schultz, D. P., & Schultz, S. E. (2008). *Theories of personality* (9th ed.). Belmont, CA: Wadsworth Cengage Learning.

Sökefeld, M. (1999). Debating self, identity, and culture in anthropology. *Current Anthropology, 40*(4), 417–448.

Stanislavski, C. (1937). *An actor prepares* (E. R. Hapgood, Trans., 8th ed.). London: Lowe & Brydone.

Storr, A. (1989). *Freud: A very short introduction*. New York: Oxford University Press.

Strasberg, L., & Schechner, R. (1964). Working with live material. *The Tulane Drama Review, 9*(1), 117–135.

Svirsky, M. (2009). "A stirring alphabet of thought: Review essay", Deleauze studies. *Research Online, University of Wollongong, 3*, 311–324.

Walton, G. (2007). A question of belonging: Race, social fit, and achievement. *Journal of Personality and Social Psychology, 92*(1), 82–96.

Winnicott, D. W. (1965). *The maturational process and the facilitating environment*. London: Hogarth Press.

Winnicott, D. W. (1989). *Psycho-analytic explorations*. Cambridge, MA: Harvard University Press.

Zandy, J. (1990). *Calling home: Working-class women's writings*. New Brunswick, NJ: Rutgers University Press.

3 Affinity with Armenia: a narrative in two parts

> I should like to see any power of the world destroy this race, this small tribe of unimportant people, whose history is ended, whose wars have all been fought and lost, whose structures have crumbled, whose literature is unread, whose music is unheard, whose prayers are no longer uttered. Go ahead, destroy this race. Let us say that it is again 1915.... See if the race will not live again.... For when two of them meet anywhere in the world, see if they will not create a New Armenia.
>
> (Saroyan, 1935, p. 438)

Part I: what went before

Birth of a nation

Much of the following narrative is translated from the history textbook *Հայոց Պատմություն* (Էլոյեան, Հայրապետեան, & Շահնազարեան, 1982), which I studied in Armenian school, and from the stories that I was taught as an adolescent. For the purposes of this book, these accounts have been relearnt and supported through the work of Armenian professor and scientist Paris M. Herouni (2004) via his book *Armenians and Old Armenia: Archaeoastronomy, Linguistics, Oldest History*. The history of Armenia has also been studied in-depth through the works of authors such as Rouben Paul Adalian (2015), Charles King (2008), Dr Clarence Ussher (1917), Simon Payaslian (2007) and Raymond Kevorikian (2011).

To say Armenia is an old country would be an understatement since the nation's history dates back to 4000 BC. Legend says that Armenia as a nation was birthed through its patriarch, Hayk. Similar to the story of David and Goliath (The Holy Bible, Sam. 17:1–58), Hayk defeated the evil Assyrian ruler Bel in a heroic battle to win his people's freedom. From then, the land that Hayk's people occupied was identified as Hayastan,[1] and a nation was born. This is simply one example of Armenia's rich, storied past, and although these legends may seem fanciful, they do correlate with documented historical events, such as the story of Saint Grigor (also known as Gregory the Illuminator). In the first Golden Age, Saint Grigor began to write the pages of Armenia's history when he converted King Trdat III to Christianity and, as a result, in 301 AD, Armenia became the first ever nation to officially establish the Christian faith (Herouni, 2004).

This momentous and symbolic religious event means that Armenians hold their faith in high esteem. They built religious fortresses within the mountainous terrains to help protect their beloved churches from any invaders and fought endlessly to keep their practices of the Christian faith in a time when the church was constantly under threat from the Arabs and Turks of that period. Even now, many Orthodox Armenian clergy believe in Armenia's sacred antiquity, maintaining the belief that, after the entombment of Jesus, His body was conveyed by angels to Mount Ararat[2] and deposited beside the remains of Noah's Ark (Gen. 8:4), which, according to them, can still be found there. As stated in *The Armenians* by C.F. Dixon-Johnson (1916):

> During the period when He made Himself visible to His disciples, as related in the New Testament, Christ again assumed this earthly body, which after His ascent to Heaven was reconveyed by the angels to Mount Ararat, where it still lies in a secret tomb, uncorrupted and ready to be reassumed once more at His second coming upon earth.
>
> (p. 7)

I recognise that, like most stories, the truth of this specific tale largely depends on the individual's religious beliefs. However, fables like these were important to the Armenian people and became a large part of *our* (Armenian) identity. As the Armenians from Armenia dispersed across the world, they carried with them these stories from their homeland. Across foreign nations, diaspora Armenians continued to share these ancient fables, and soon the stories became embedded within the philosophy of the Armenian culture. Travelling over many generations, these tales became the bedtime stories communicated to me and helped form my Armenian cultural identity. This experience resonates with most Armenians. In *Contemporary Armenian American Drama: An Anthropology*, Professor Nishan Parlakian (2004) observed how successful contemporary Armenian playwrights and novelists have used their natural impulses as storytellers to combine their culture with their deep need to tell stories. Parlakian discussed how this tendency is a habitual compulsion that has been cultivated over time and over many generations. He observed that, in a way, the storytelling provides a means to ensure that Armenian ethnic identity and traditions, encompassed by their faith, endure and that the "feared dissolution of their racial individuality through assimilations, is evaded" (pp. 3–5). The assimilations to which Parlakian is referring are the follow-on effects of the agonies associated with the Armenian Genocide. The transference of these stories from their homeland was a desperate attempt by diaspora Armenians to keep hold of their ethnicity while undergoing the turmoil of constant upheaval.

In the fourth century AD, Armenian priests quickly adopted this desire for storytelling. They understood that Armenians had a profound need to share and acquire knowledge. The priests soon recognised that, for the people to be able to document and share this information, "written language" was needed. For the priests themselves, the development of a written language was the logical progression. It was important that the documentation of their wisdom and knowledge be available to all Armenian people. In the latter part of the fourth century AD, the priests eventually came across a devoted Armenian monk named Meshrob Mashtots who studied foreign languages, and with the sanction of the church, they enlisted him to invent an alphabet that reflected the pronunciations of the Armenian tongue. With the aid of his students, Mashtots travelled far and wide, gathering the sounds of the current spoken language, resulting, in 405 AD, in the 36 characters that form the basis of the Armenian alphabet (Herouni, 2004). This achievement was profound, as not only did Mashtots go on to build schools all across Armenia but also his alphabet became the basis of all Indo-European languages (Herouni, 2004). This accomplishment would successfully set forth Armenia's course from the Golden Ages.

The beginnings of the invaders

Armenia's transition from the Golden Ages into the next period was not an undisturbed one. Geographically, Armenia was situated at a deadly intersection between Turkey, Persia[3] and Assyria. As far back as the Roman Empire era, Armenia's geographical position had always been high on the radar of its neighbouring countries. In the seventh century, Armenia was eventually taken over by the Arabs, who, because of Armenia's topographical positioning, believed it was a perfect crossroads between the Western and Eastern divides. Therefore, Armenia suffered many onslaughts during this period while under Arab rule. It was not until the ninth century when the Bagratid Dynasty[4] overtook Armenia that Armenia managed to escape from Arab rule, and so, with that dynasty's reign, the country began to progress into its second Golden Age.

A monk named Gregory (Narekatsi, 1977) documented this period of prosperity in his book of prayers, discussing how the Bagratid Dynasty broke Armenia free from strict Arab rule, brought about peace and assisted Armenia in developing as a nation, both architecturally and creatively. Between the ninth and tenth centuries, Armenia reaped the rewards of its new enrichments, but its inhabitants did not realise that in the eleventh century, the Seljik Turks would devastate the country once again.

The Seljik Turks fought their way through Armenia against the Persians, using Armenia's mountainous terrains as a battlefield and inflicting destruction on the country. In conjunction with the onset of the Mongols in the thirteenth century, a succession of invasions continued to ravage the country. During this chaos, the Armenian kingdom diminished and was forced to the shores of the Mediterranean Sea, where it survived until the fourteenth century. After Constantinople fell to the Ottoman Empire, the Ottomans overtook what was left of Armenia in the sixteenth century. However, the Persians also laid claim to Armenian soil, and the two adversaries eventually settled their differences by splitting Armenia between their two empires, although as the Russian Empire began to rise to power in the nineteenth century, the Persian share of the empire diminished. At this time, Eastern Armenia relinquished power to Russia under the Turkmanchay Treaty and remained that way until the twentieth century (King, 2008). The turn of the twentieth century was, in my view, the beginning of Armenia's most profound moment in history, when the onslaught of new invaders to the country was set in motion.

The Armenian Genocide

Despite the endless onslaught of invaders, over time, Armenia achieved many historical accomplishments. However, if there is one historical event that stands out in the minds of every Armenian, both young and old, it is the devastation of 24 April 1915, which forever changed the course of Armenian history. The massacres carried out from 1915 to 1918, widely known as the "Armenian Genocide", are events that we, as a nation and as a civilisation, can never, and will never, forget.

In the late 1800s, as Sultan Hamid II began ruling the Ottoman Empire, so began Armenia's bloodshed. During this time, the Ottoman Empire was looking to implement reforms all across Eastern Europe and wanted conformity of the ethnic groups involved. Sultan Hamid II demanded that his tenet be taken seriously and decided the best way to set forth on this course of action was to make an example of one ethnic group, the most devoted of the populace. In 1896, he ordered the massacre of 300,000 Armenians as an illustration of the seriousness of his decree to the rest of the citizens in the surrounding regions (El-Ghusein, 1918). This dictate was only the beginning of what would become the darkest page in Armenia's history.

Despite the Sultan's warning, by the turn of the century, the Ottoman Turks' protective boundaries were continuing to shrink. Fearing their empire would collapse into oblivion, a group of educated Turks (later known as the "Young Turks") formed a group to overturn Sultan Hamid II and take power over the country. However, the promised reforms failed. Out of options in the midst of the First World War, the Young Turks allied themselves with Germany. On 24 April 1915, the Young Turks gathered a group of intellectual leaders from the Armenian community and, with no reason or warning, executed them in public. Next, they turned their attention to the Armenian people and the terrain on which they had been living for centuries. A horrific bloodstained massacre ensued, involving the rape of women in front of their children, children slaughtered in front of their mothers and men butchered in front of their wives. Those who did survive the Young Turks' carnage were starved, fatigued and later forced to dig their own graves before their mass killing (Bonjukian Patten, 2015). These massacres became known as the Armenian Genocide.

Dr Clarence Ussher (1917), who at the time of the annihilations was a medical missionary in Van,[5] wrote detailed accounts of the exterminations in his memoirs, *An American Physician in Turkey*:

> Women had been thrown into the heated clay ovens in the ground, kerosene poured over them and ignited and worse things had been done . . . throughout the province at that very hour thousands of defenceless men, women, and children were being slaughtered with the utmost brutality. Turkish soldiers had been quartered in every Armenian village with instructions to begin at a certain hour. The general order read: "The Armenians must be exterminated".
> (pp. 58, 244)

Although there is extensive first-hand documentation of the events in the lead-up to and during the genocide (Ahnert, 2007; Miller & Miller, 1999; Svazlian, 2011;

Ussher, 1917), it is not clear how the Armenian Genocide actually ended. It is rumoured in historical literature (Adalian, 2015; Hovhannisyan & Mardanyan, 2012; Kifner, 2014; Sassounian, 2014; Smith, Markusen, & Lifton, 1995) that the Ottoman/Turkish Empire's final acceptance of defeat after World War I effectively ended Turkish control of the Armenians and, in turn, ended the massacres in 1918. By the end of 1923, estimations calculated that close to two million Armenians had been murdered under the direct actions of the ruling Turks. At the time, the effect of the Armenian Genocide was so significant that, over 20 years later, Hitler would use the Armenian Genocide as a motivational ploy in his Obersalzberg Speech delivered on 22 August 1939 as part of his Final Solution. Hitler famously proclaimed, "Who, after all, speaks to-day of the annihilation of the Armenians?" (as cited in Lochner, 1942, p. 4).

Even in the face of documentary evidence, to this day, the Turkish government has refused Armenians recognition of the massacres of 1915. For decades, Turkish leaders have been under increasing pressure from the international communities to admit culpability for the killings and face their country's past. During a visit to Turkey in January of 2014, French President François Hollande, without using the word "genocide", called on Turkish leaders to confront their history, stating,

> Memory work is always painful . . . but must be done. What we need is to carry out reconciliation through research and recognition of what has happened. . . . By recognizing the historical events you will be elevated not only in your own eyes, but also in the eyes of the world.
> (as cited in Sassounian, 2014, p. 1)

President Hollande's call for acknowledgement is only one of the many appeals that have come from official representatives. American President Bill Clinton (1994) acknowledged the actualisation of the genocide on 22 April 1994 by saying,

> On this solemn day, I join Armenians from around the world in remembering the victims of the 1915 massacres in the Ottoman Empire. The effects of that tragedy have profoundly touched all of us, and together we mourn the terrible loss of so many innocent lives.
> (p. 1)

As did American President Barack Obama, who said,

> Today we commemorate the *Meds Yeghern* [great catastrophe] and honor those who perished in one of the worst atrocities of the 20th century. Ninety-eight years ago, 1.5 million Armenians were massacred or marched to their deaths in the final days of the Ottoman Empire.
> ("Obama commemorates 'Meds Yeghern'", 2013, para. 1)

However, although Clinton and Obama acknowledged the massacres of 1915, both avoided the word genocide in their speeches. Conversations once again began in the United States in 2019, and on 30 October 2019, the US House of Representatives voted overwhelmingly to recognise the Armenian Genocide of a century ago, placing tension on the current US-Turkey relationship (Gambino, 2019). However, despite the defiance of both US President Donald Trump and Turkish President Recap Tayyip Erdoğan, on 12 December 2019, the US Senate finally cast a unanimous vote to recognise the genocide of the Armenians by the Ottoman Empire (Borger, 2019). This recognition from the US Senate was a symbolic victory for Armenian Americans, as it marked the culmination of more than 50 years of relentless campaigning.

Some may argue that what happened over 100 years ago bears no meaning today and, therefore, the ongoing attempts to bring about recognition should be forgotten. However, I am confident that although there are many Armenians who have had the ability to forget or forgive what happened in 1915, few have been prepared to do so. I have often asked myself, "How is it that the occurrences of this event still affect me today?", and "Why has the Genocide continually remained a focal fixity throughout my life when it happened over a century ago and most of my descendants came from New Julfa[6] in Persia?" The answer is often that I do not understand why; all I do know is that the incident remains a prominent subject in my life as an Armenian and as a storyteller. The empathy I hold for *my people* not only affects my individual identity but also influences my work as a director, to the point where, in most cases, the knowledge of the genocide and its irresolution have made me sensitive to conflict issues.

Associate Professor Amy Cook (2011) observed empathy in-depth and considered that empathy is a relationship that occurs when pain, cognition and interpretation act together, and thus it becomes a full-bodied experience. She explained the many reasons for empathy, including the desire to do something for the other person in the relationship – a reflection that resonates powerfully with me. It stems from the deep desire to gain justice for those who perished under this gruesome act by achieving recognition of their deaths. I am aware that the antipathy I feel towards the *enemy* is reflective of the fact that, to this day, Turkey has not shown empathy or claimed ownership of the genocide committed in 1915. Further, I recognise that, although my bitterness towards modern Turkey today may seem misplaced and unjust, and is by no means something I intentionally seek out, regrettably, the empathy within me for the assassinated Armenians habitually transfers to, and expresses itself equally as, hostility towards the murderers. It is effortless for the oppressors to say that the event should be forgotten; it is a different matter altogether for its victims.

In his book *An Inconvenient Genocide: Who Now Remembers the Armenians?*, Australian Queen's counsel Geoffrey Robertson (2014) discussed extensively the controversial denial of the Armenian Genocide and that while 32 parliaments in democratic countries have voted to recognise the genocide, Britain and Australia continue to vacillate or even avoid the subject for fear of estranging their North Atlantic Treaty Organization allies. Through eyewitness accounts by Australian prisoners of war, who at the time were fighting the Turks themselves, Robertson's book proves beyond reasonable doubt that the horrific events of 1915 constitute a crime against humanity and, therefore, should be officially recognised as genocide. In the lead-up to its centenary, Robertson (2009, 2010, 2014) remained an avid vocal supporter of this recognition. As such, in January 2015, when legalities finally began in the European Court of Human Rights (ECHR) to cease the denial of the genocide officially and bring about its recognition, Robertson, alongside prominent human rights barrister Amal Alamuddin Clooney, represented Armenia on behalf of Doughty Street Chambers. In their opening speech, Alamuddin Clooney articulated the importance of this trial:

> Armenia must have its day in court. . . . The stakes could not be higher for the Armenian people. I share the pain of Armenian citizens, you can not find a word of mine that expresses antagonism against them. I hold the great powers responsible for what happened in 1915. There should be no taboos for the right to speak.
> (as cited in Waterfield, 2015, p. 1)

As 24 April 2015 approached, Armenians from all across the world waited in anticipation to see what the results of the trial would be and if *they* would finally receive recognition of the genocide from the Turkish governing powers. Leading up to the day, several high-profile figures spoke out about the genocide and demanded acknowledgement of that term. Pope Francis echoed the words of the late Pope John Paul II and, at a special memorial at St Peter's Basilica, said that the Armenian Genocide was the first genocide of the twentieth century. He added,

> We recall the centenary of that tragic event, that immense and senseless slaughter whose cruelty your forebears had to endure. It is necessary, and indeed a duty, to honour their memory, for whenever memory fades, it means that evil allows wounds to fester.
> (as cited in Scammell, 2015, para. 8)

Of course, Pope Francis's description of the mass killings of the Armenians 100 years ago as genocide did not resonate well with the Turkish government. It was rumoured that his pronouncement may have politically explosive repercussions, which could damage diplomatic relations with Turkey in the near future (Scammell, 2015).

On 15 April 2015, the European Union adopted a resolution commemorating the centennial of the Armenian Genocide and urged Turkey to recognise the events (European Parliament, 2015). On 24 April 2015, all over the world, the Armenian diaspora, 24 other nations (now 32), which still does not include Australia, stood to recognise the events that occurred in 1915 as genocide – without the quotation marks. They stood to commemorate the centenary of the murder of over one-and-a-half million Armenians at the hands of the Ottoman Turkish government. However, despite numerous facts, photos, certifications and authoritarian documentations, Turkey continues to deny the genocide ever happened. As the court case to bring about recognition of the Armenian Genocide is still proceeding in the ECHR, Armenians from all over the world still live in hope.

The Republic of Armenia today

Taking leave of the mayhem from its past and the refutation of the genocide, on 23 August 1990, following the disablement of the Soviet Union, Armenia declared independence, becoming the first non-Baltic republic to separate from the Union. However, it is important to note that, in fact, Armenia did not officially receive formal independence until late in 1991.

Armenia's post-Soviet years were plagued with hardship due to economic difficulties, as well as the eruption, in 1993, of a full-scale armed battle between the Karabakh Armenians and Azerbaijan. Turkey once again joined the blockade against Armenia in support of Azerbaijan, leaving Armenians isolated and fending for themselves. In 1994, after further bloodshed, the Nagorno-Karabakh War finally ended, as Russia negotiated a ceasefire that has held, precariously, to this day. However, although the war was in some way positive for Armenia (which was victorious), by the time the ceasefire was agreed upon, an estimated 300,000 Armenians were said to have been killed (Cornell, 1999).

Optimistically speaking, as difficult and as destructive as the restoration of independence was for Armenia, it did set in motion economic freedoms and industrial productions that proudly culminated in what is recognised today as the Republic of Armenia. As the Republic of Armenia advances with its reforms to forge its identity within the world, its battles with Turkey and the surrounding neighbours remain a constant threat. Armenia's current situation echoes the now famous words of William Saroyan (1935), one of Armenia's most beloved playwrights and authors,

> I should like to see any power of the world destroy this race, this small tribe of unimportant people. . . . See if the race will not live again. . . . For when two of them meet anywhere in the world, see if they will not create a New Armenia.
> (p. 438)

This excerpt from Saroyan's legacy is sustained in my mind as I think about the ever-changeable future of Armenia.

In 2018, a series of anti-government protests that were staged by various political and civil groups led by now Prime Minister Nikol Pashinyan caused a monumental movement in Armenia that was known as the "Velvet Revolution" (Demytire, 2018). The month-long revolt would go on to oust Armenia's twice serving prime minister and third president Serzh Sargsyan and, inherently, the Republican-controlled government that had been in place since Armenia's independence in 1990. By the time 22 April 2018 arrived, an estimated 500,000 demonstrators had packed Republic Square in Yerevan city demanding Sargsyan's resignation. As the flag-waving campaigners held their ground, Sargsyan was left with no choice but to finally end his controversial reign. This uprising, which was won by the people without any violence or bloodshed, finally raised *real* hopes of impartiality and justice for Armenia and its people.

Against formidable odds, the country has already come far, but I recognise how far it still has to go. As Armenia makes its way through the twenty-first century under the new Pashinyan administration, adversities and demands for recognition of the massacres of the past remain a pivotal impediment to its economic, geographical and emotional progress.

My voyage from a dream to reality

September 2008

Travelling to Armenia for the first time was a momentous occasion. As a young adolescent, I had imagined that someday I would have the opportunity to visit Armenia and experience what it would be like to step foot on my "homeland".[7] Ironically, as bell hooks (2009) suggested in *Kentucky Is My Fate*, living away from my "native" place had, over time, made Armenia something of a constructed memory, so when the opportunity finally presented itself in September 2008, I was overjoyed. That year, I had read an interview with actor-musician Cher, who, upon travelling to Armenia for the first time, said,

> Growing up, everyone in my family was light, blonde, green eyed, except me. So, when I arrived in Armenia, I turned around and thought everybody looks like me here. That was a real discovery for me. Yes, I am Armenian. I finally realized I belonged.
>
> (as cited in Chaderjian, 2008)

Growing up, I knew all too well that Cher and I shared the same dilemma. Both of us were Armenian females trying to exist within the confines of a Western world. I yearned for that same experience of belonging that Cher felt, and I was convinced that feelings identical to hers would envelop me as soon as I arrived in my homeland. However, when I did arrive, the sense of acceptance that Cher felt and for which I longed quickly dispersed.

Within my first days of arriving in Armenia, when continually questioned about where I was from, my reply remained the same: "Australia". Instantaneously, the Armenian people began to counter with, "Then you are not Armenian; you were not born here; you did not grow up here and suffer through the country's hardship like we did". I was heartbroken. Of course I was Armenian. I may not have been born or bred in Armenia, but my parents were Armenian, I knew how to read and write the language, and I had been nurtured in all its traditions. This response continued throughout my stay. While excited when arriving in Armenia, I left feeling dejected. All the years of built-up anticipation of the positive experiences I would have in Armenia were immediately yanked out from under me, as the unhomely moment slowly crept upon me (Bhabha, 1992). In the eyes of the Armenian people, I was the *other*. I was not an Armenian but an outsider. To them, I was simply another tourist, there to take happy snaps and pose among the iconic locations. As I tried hopelessly to fit in as a true Armenian and not be the *other*, not even my desperate attempts to disguise my Persian-Armenian-Australian dialect could succeed in deceiving them. The Armenia in which I had stored my memory was a mere "imaginary homeland" (Rushdie, 1992) that bore little resemblance to the authentic Armenia I was witnessing first-hand. I was hurt. The rejection by the Armenian people I met left me feeling bitter.

After two weeks in Yerevan, the time finally came to leave. Anxious to depart, I woke up early that morning and could not wait until we arrived at the airport. What I did not realise at the time was that, at the airport, I would once again have to endure further humiliation that would leave me loathing the Armenian populace even more.

While we waited in line to check in our bags, a security guard came up to my parents and me and demanded that we wait for the woman at counter three. At the time, I remember thinking what a bizarre request that was, as an alternative counter was free. However, he was a figure of authority and remained insistent, so we listened. Eventually, our time came, and we proceeded to the counter. At the desk, an edgy-looking woman weighed our bags and, soon after, alleged that our bags were over the standard acceptable weight. I immediately disagreed with her, confident that all our bags were well under the required weight. Yet she persisted and said that if we wanted to board the plane, we needed to pay cash for the additional excess.

"How much?" I asked.

"How much do you have?" she replied.

Instantly, I recognised that something suspect was befalling us. My level of disappointment with the country had now escalated in a way I could never have predicted.

On the flight back to Australia, I said to my father, "If this is how narrow-minded and thievish *real* Armenians are, then I am ashamed to be one". We would hear several stories – experiences of our Sydney Armenian acquaintances – resembling what had happened to us at the airport. It seemed these experiences were frequent. In fact, a friend of our family told us that when he was exiting Armenia, the officers at the airport challenged his passport, saying that it was not authentic. He told them, "It was authentic enough for you to let me into the country". However, it seemed the guards had now changed their minds. Our friend then replied, "So tell me, how much will it cost for the passport to become authentic again?" Needleless to say, after some "negotiations", the matter was resolved.

In time, my father saw how much that trip had affected me and explained that I should not take the Armenians' reactions too much to heart, as they were a population that had only received full independence in late 1991, exiting what had been a strict communist regime. The changes after the fall of the Soviet Union left the majority of the people in Armenia jobless, distraught, poor and living in horrendous conditions. For a long time, Armenia had a limited water supply, no heat and a scarcity of food; the bitterness of their ways was a result of the frustration brought on by these conditions and other significant events. It seems that when they saw an Armenian who had not lived through the hardship and despair they had endured, they could not help expressing their aggravation towards that individual. Nonetheless, even though in time I did learn to recognise the truth in my father's words, the bitterness I had developed towards them never went away. I often found myself recalling my experiences in Armenia, and while a part of me felt saddened for the country, the people and their past, for some reason, I could not bring myself to erase my unpleasant memories of the voyage. It seemed that, in the two short weeks I was there, the authenticity of my Armenian heritage was stolen from me and, once again, my sense of belonging in the world was lost.

Part II: the journey back

> Year 1992. . . . An Armennian [sic] young man, aggrieved with all the World, tried to remember the truth which was forgotten by his nation. He came to far Tibet, hoping to find his soul teacher. He roamed for a long time, hungry and thirsty. After long searching, broken down and covered with wounds, he at last saw a lama, who was plunged in prayer with closed eyes. Around him the snow and ice have melded due to his huge energy. Lama opened his eyes and smiling said at once: "What have you lost in these lands, the mad son of the Sun?" Then he cured the Armennian's [sic] wounds and some days later, when parting, he told him: "The source of truth you are looking for so long time, is in your beautiful country called Armennia [sic], which is the cradle of civilization. You are the first Aryans. You forgot about that, but your enemies remember it. I can teach you nothing, the knowledge is inside you. Go back to your country and you will find the truth in your wonderful mountains."
>
> (A. M. Avvettissyan, as cited in Herouni, 2004, p. 236)

September 2014

In 2014, and much like the young man in Herouni's story, I felt a compelling need to remember the truth of my story, which had been magnified by my PhD research. I identified that, to rediscover my position as a person and a theatre director-researcher and to probe deeper into my attitude towards my cultural inheritance as a Persian-Armenian-Australian, I had to return to my "homeland" of Armenia. Over time, I had learnt to understand the behaviours of the various individuals I had encountered on my first visit; the wounds, however, still ran deep. I found it not so simple to forgive and forget, and therefore, I anticipated the worst.

Resistant and half-hearted, I made the unenthusiastic journey back, and as the time came to board the flight, I sensed myself defiant at every step. Rebellious and determined to maintain the charade, this time as an Australian, as I entered the gates at Zvartnots Airport, I refused to speak a word of Armenian. I conversed in English only, my logic being that if I did not come across as an Armenian, "they" could not hurt me, thus building a shield between "them" and me. The absurdity was that everything about me screamed Armenian: my black hair, my dark eyes, not to mention my name – one of the most nationalistic Armenian names there is. At border security, one of the officers questioned my status.

"Հայերէն չե՞ս կարող խոսիլ", she said.

"No", I responded, "I don't know how to speak Armenian".

"Հայ չե՞ս", she challenged.

Lying, I replied, "Yes, I am Armenian but I can't speak it" and quickly ended the contest. I felt so stupid. I could see that she did not believe a word I'd said.

Exiting the airport, I felt embarrassed and disgusted with myself. What was I trying to prove?

After a good night's sleep, renewed, I awoke recalling my "performance" at the airport. The shame had still not left me. I was so determined that this time around the homeland would not wound me, I did not realise that I was now placing myself in a position that sabotaged any hope of an altered experience. In my mind, I had created a barrier between "us" and "them" – "us" referring to *me* the non-native and "them" being the inhabitants of the land – and, in turn, my bizarre act at the airport proved this. The anxiety of my past interactions with the Armenian people had affected me so deeply that I had not understood that now I was *othering* myself yet again. American psychiatrist Aaron Temkin Beck and his associates proposed that we all have deep cognitive structures in our memory called schemas and that these can be activated by stressful events, which force us to interpret our experiences in a particularly significant way (Beck & Beck, 2011). As noted in the publication *The Case Formulation Approach to Cognitive-Behavior Therapy* (Persons, 2008), although Beck's cognitive theory was initially proposed as an account of depression, his theories have been adapted to incorporate any event that may be connected to an extensive range of problems, including anxiety brought on by past occurrences in an individual's memory. This interpretative lens might be perceived as a protective mechanism. Was that what had happened to me? Had my past experiences affected my memory so profoundly that now my logic was trying to interpret and create a new response to protect me? Either way, at that moment, I recognised that if I did not quickly adjust or change my automatic reactions to the situation, no matter what wonderful events might transpire on this second trip, I would undoubtedly be disinclined to notice them. Therefore, I paid attention to my attitude and put the previous trip behind me. I reminded myself that what had transpired in 2008 had already occurred, and while the upsets were overwhelming at the time, I could not change the past. However, I could allow myself to appreciate any new experiences that might await me.

A New Armenia or a new me?

In six years, there had been considerable change in Armenia. It was not so much a transformation of the countryside or the city of Yerevan itself – the people were different. In contrast to my experiences in 2008, this time, the people were polite and welcoming. The negative manner and brashness of the Armenians, which was one of the major impediments that I encountered the previous time, had faded. Instead, the people looked awakened and appeared ready for a transformation of some sort. After conversing with many Armenians whom I casually met in Yerevan, I quickly developed the impression that the people, especially the youth, were fed up with the politics surrounding their country. The Armenian people seemed more aware of the negative impressions that travellers might take with them when they left the country. This awareness might have been initiated by the large increase of tourism in Armenia over the past couple of years ("Number of foreign tourists", 2014) and consequently increased consciousness of the image

56 *Affinity with Armenia*

that they projected to the rest of the world. As it turned out, my assumptions were not too far from reality.

Prior to the country's 2018 historic revolution, on 10 October 2014, over 100,000 citizens attended a rally in Yerevan's Freedom Square, demanding change from the government concerning the corruption that had infiltrated the city since the Soviet years. Maria Titizian, managing editor of CivilNet, an independent online TV station, said that besides the large number of protesters who turned up, challenging the administrative bodies, what made the rally unusual was that three parties from Armenia's normally fragmented opposition had come together to show their support (as cited in Wikstrom, 2014). Titizian added, "We've come to a point where a majority of the population is really dissatisfied with the quality of living and the level of impunity and corruption, and they're desperate for change" (as cited in Wikstrom, 2014, para. 6). It was evident that even then, gradually, the Republic of Armenia and its people were progressively changing and, as an Armenian, I perceived this as positive for the future of the country.

I am not sure if it was these unexpected alterations in Armenia or if it was the shame following my disgraceful arrival, but my connection to and within Armenia was special this time around. Although I inevitably played the role of the tourist, I experienced aspects of Armenia that only a few "tourists" receive the opportunity to see. Most of these experiences occurred on my travels within Armenia, as I often left the city of Yerevan and headed towards the small villages that surrounded the capital city. These expeditions were something I was not able to pursue on my previous visit. Travelling across the picturesque and mountainous landscapes of Armenia and being overwhelmed by the wealth of history produced emotions that, even now, I struggle to articulate. However, while all these instances had a hand in helping me rediscover the significance of my cultural identity, a particularly special occasion occurred when I travelled south to the country of Karabakh (also known as Artsakh in Armenian), now recognised as the Nagorno-Karabakh Republic.

While the history of Nagorno-Karabakh is long and difficult to explain in a couple of paragraphs, what is important to note about this special country is that, over time, the Armenian people have shed much blood, sweat and tears to regain control over this small region of land. Throughout history, Karabakh has been in the hands of many nations, but predominantly, it has remained an Armenian state. Unfortunately, due to its geographical positioning, over time, it saw countless conflicts: "The Azeris claim that the region has always been under Azeri rule in known history; by contrast the Armenians advance the claim that Karabakh was originally an Armenian site of residence and that Azeri rule was illegitimate" (Cornell, 1999, p. 3). During the Soviet years, both Armenia and Georgia at some juncture were taken over by the Bolsheviks. The Bolsheviks, to gain public support, assured the Armenians that one day they would give Karabakh to them. What the Armenians did not realise at the time of the guarantee was that, on a bigger scale, Moscow had other plans involving Turkey and, therefore, broke its promises and transferred Karabakh to Azerbaijan (Cornell, 1999; Torosyan, 2012).

Since the Soviet time, the nations of Azerbaijan and Armenia have been in continual conflict over the province of Karabakh. In 1923, because of the constant unrest still reported in Karabakh, discussions took place over the status of Karabakh within Azerbaijan until finally a decision was made to give the region the rank of an autonomous state called Oblast. The Oblast included the mountainous part of Karabakh and consequently was called the Nagorno-Karabakh Autonomous Oblast, hereafter known as the NKAO (Cornell, 1999, p. 3). However, while the ethnically Armenian citizens of that region lived under the reign of the NKAO for over 60 years, they never ceased trying to gain repossession of "their land". Ultimately, in 1991, the early stages of the Nagorno-Karabakh War began. Svante Cornell (1999) wrote in his book *The Nagorno-Karabakh Conflict*,

> By early 1992 the power vacuum created by the dissolution of the Soviet Union led to the loss of the last factor containing the conflict. Thus with the imminent withdrawal of the formerly Soviet forces, Karabakh became the scene of what gradually increased to a full-scale war. The Armenian side, having prepared itself to solve the conflict through military means, did not lose any time to act.
>
> (p. 9)

Accordingly, aggressive fighting started and continued into early 1994. Although in the beginning it was reported that Azerbaijani forces were winning various battles, by May 1994, the Armenians were in control of 20 per cent of the Azerbaijani terrain, and for the first time, the Government of Azerbaijan saw Nagorno-Karabakh as a third party of the war and in desperation began direct negotiations with the Karabakhi authorities. As a result of the negotiations, an unofficial ceasefire was reached on 12 May 1994, and that ceasefire continues to this day, with Nagorno-Karabakh under the control of the Armenian military. After many years of war and many thousands of people being killed, in 1994, the Azerbaijanis were officially driven out of Nagorno-Karabakh, as well as the territories neighbouring the region (Cornell, 1999; Torosyan, 2012).

Being submerged in all this history, which I had learnt and relearnt through texts and stories recounted in my teenage years, made this expedition to Karabakh much more significant for me. It was as if an overwhelming connection to the land and the Armenian soil, which was in some way absent from both my visits to Yerevan, had suddenly enveloped me in Karabakh.

Driving through the Lachin corridor[8] was a surreal experience. I had heard about this "corridor" growing up and had heard that if Armenian soldiers had not gained control over the area, there was a great chance that the Republic of Armenia today would not be ours. Visiting Karabakh and seeing the repercussions from the 1992 battles left me with such diverse feelings: extreme pride because of the Armenian soldiers who had fought unwaveringly to give us back part of our history, sadness because of the real-life stories heard via the women who had lost sons, brothers and fathers in the conflicts and then tremendous fear of what the future might bring – as the presence of the Azerbaijanis was still very near. While in Karabakh, I stayed in Stepanakert, the capital and largest city. I journeyed through various villages surrounding the city, arriving at Shushi, and saw where the most significant parts

58 Affinity with Armenia

of the 1992 war were fought and won. However, although these were all wonderful experiences, the time I spent in the small village of Tsaghkadzor left the most profound and unexpected impression on me.

In Tsaghkadzor, I spent the day with a woman named Laora who lived in a home iconic to the traditional villages that surrounded her. Her food and drink came from the land and the animals she cared for, and her house was so different from what I was accustomed to that immediately it prompted images in my mind of what ancient Armenia might have looked like (see Figure 3.1). At first, taken aback and reluctant in my behaviour towards her and my surroundings, my misguided naïve Westerner's judgement caused me to think, "Poor lady, she has so little", but that perspective was flawed. I learnt that her eldest son had been killed in the Nagorno-Karabakh War, and I met her neighbours, who had shared similar fates with loved ones dying in the war.

Just seeing the pride in the villagers and the deep love for what they had instead of dismay at what they did not have astonished me. Further, the forgiveness they possessed for the Azerbaijanis when they spoke of their loved ones who had perished made me feel so ashamed. "These are the true Armenians", I thought. "I am not a true Armenian; I am a fraud. I am a fly-in-fly-out Armenian. An imitation of one, who walks around reciting the history and speaking of the animosity for Turkey, but in front of me are the living breathing examples of what being an Armenian is all about". I realised that I was an Armenian when it suited me and an Australian the rest of the time; how could I have possibly compared my affections for my ethnicity to those of the people who lived and unconditionally treasured it day in and day out?

The feeling of my deception followed me as I made my way back to the city of Yerevan. I recalled all the moments when I tried so hard to shed my Armenian features and traditions and conform to what my idea of an Australian was because

Figure 3.1 Laora's kitchen, pantry, spare room and front yard in Tsaghkadzor (2014)
Photographer: Soseh Yekanians

I was so ashamed of my difference. I remembered all the times I spoke badly about *my* people and did not think twice about how life was and is for Armenians living in Armenia with the daily unrest. With all the duplicity in my life, what gave me the right to call myself an Armenian? Laora had a right to call herself an Armenian, but what was my claim? The language I spoke, the traditions I was raised in, my faith? I wondered if this was all part of my subconscious confusion growing up, which ultimately led to my sense of displacement and pursuit of conforming to a certain sense of identity. If so, did other young Armenians in Armenia share similar thoughts or was this exclusively for those who were not inhabitants of the homeland?

Hasmik Ter Karapetyan-Chater, a theatre lecturer at the Yerevan State Institute of Theatre and Cinema in Armenia, believes that this fragmented sense of identity that so many Armenians hold is due to the unresolved circumstances still left within Armenian history (personal communication, 12 September 2014). I consider that she may be right. In his book *On Apology*, Aaron Lazare (2005) wrote about how an apology's significance lies in the dual role it plays for both the victim and the offender. He notes that an apology provides victims with recognition and allows for grievance, but at the same time, it offers offenders the opportunity not only to make amends but also to accept responsibility for their actions, thus providing some kind of closure for all involved. The apology is often the first step. As an Armenian, I have no doubt that this gesture is exactly what *we* as a nation need to provide at least the beginnings of some form of healing for the Armenian people. However, I wondered how this issue affects the youth in Armenia today. Is it as prominent in their lives as it is in mine, and does it affect their sense of identity? Following a presentation that I gave at the Yerevan State Institute of Theatre and Cinema in Armenia regarding my research and the questions that I was exploring concerning my identity and strained allegiance towards my Armenian heritage, with the assistance of Ms Ter Karapetyan-Chater, I organised a question-and-answer session with a group of the students who attended the presentation and talked to them about the queries that I had. At first, I thought that my conversations would prove superfluous, as all the students were born, raised and lived in Armenia and, therefore, would not have that sense of displacement or concerns surrounding their identities that I had. However, I was surprised to discover that the young students did in fact have a fragmented sense of self and, further, of what their purpose or role within their society was meant to be.

The students, whose ages ranged between 17 and 20, spoke of the complications of growing up in a country that had achieved independence only in the past 22 years. Their parents' and grandparents' pasts predominantly comprised the Soviet years, and the students articulated how difficult it is to live in a country that on paper holds so many promises but in reality delivers so few. For them, the struggle surrounding their identities lay not so much within their nationality per se but in their lack of opportunity to question or explore it. One of the students said,

> I am Armenian, I mean, that's all there is. Even if I feel different from my parents and want to question things surrounding who I am, I can't. Where would I do it and whom would I speak to? We don't talk about those things here.
> (personal communication, 12 September 2014)

I asked her if she would investigate or question her Armenian identity if she had the opportunity to do so. She replied, "Yes, I would love to, I think we all would".

Trailing her, another student, directing her response to me, said, "You know you question your identity as an Armenian and apologise for the way you speak [talking about my mixed Persian-Armenian-Australian dialect] but I think you are more Armenian than me, than any of us here" (personal communication, 12 September 2014).

That afternoon, filled with pride, I could not shift that girl's comment from my mind. How could she think that I was more Armenian than *them*, and what if she was right? What made me continually adopt the attitude that I was any less of an Armenian? Why did I always make myself inferior to the "native" Armenian when in Armenia? I knew the history as well as *they* did – if not more. I spoke the language and loved the influence of its culture as much as *they* did – if not more. More importantly, I had enforced a period of bottomless examination concerning my existing loyalties to the culture – had *they*? Contemplating these thoughts, I immediately thought of Canadian-Armenian filmmaker Atom Egoyan.

In 2008, I read an article about Egoyan in the *Turkish Weekly* (Laciner, 2008), which stated that in his youth, he had ignored his Armenian heritage and lived like a "normal" Canadian. For a long time, he was so hostile towards his Armenian identity that he refused even to learn how to speak the language (Laciner, 2008). Reflecting back to those times, Egoyan considered that his hostility was due to living in an area where there were no other Armenians, and the people were (at the time) impervious to foreigners. Egoyan said,

> During my childhood I was desperate to assimilate, in Victoria [Canada], I wanted to be like the other kids. They used to call me the little Arab boy because I was a little darker, had a strange name and came from Egypt.
> (as cited in Laciner, 2008, p. 1)

After distancing himself from his ethnic identity for so many years and then rediscovering it in his adult years at university, Egoyan discovered that being an Armenian was not something to be ashamed of. Once Egoyan accepted his dual identity, his dramatic transformation, both as a film director and as an individual, took place and ultimately led to his success as a filmmaker (Laciner, 2008). Had I subconsciously shared the same fate? So desperate to be like the other kids around me, had I suppressed my affections and deep pride for my culture so much that, as a result, I had strayed too far? Maybe I *was* more Armenian than I ever allowed myself to envisage.

With an understanding of my resistance and attitude when I initially entered Armenia, through the expedition to Karabakh, the time spent with Laora and my conversations with the young students at the institute, I had been reintroduced to what *our* culture was principally about. Further, the desperation to find a home had slightly diminished. I began to reflect on philosophers of the romantic era, such as Friedrich Nietzsche (1996), who thought we as human beings were meant to live as wanderers. Like travellers, we wander on the earth, not drawn by destination but through observation and, therefore, should take pleasure in impermanence and change. To Nietzsche, the notion of "finding a home" would be unnatural. Instead, he would suggest that human beings need to be free of fixity in order to grow. Of course, I could appreciate how a search for home and identity, or the necessity of belonging, is significant in a person's life, but what if, similar to Hegel's (2003) notion of *self*, home and identity are evolving concepts that occur via changes or interruptions in the individual's environment? Perhaps, then, the abrupt fluctuations of *home* as setting and *identity* as a way of existing are just as important to one's development of self. If that is the case, then being the wanderer or the *in-between* would not be an undesirable position but the ideal.

Notes

1 Hayastan, derived from the legend of Hayk, is the common name used by Armenians when referring to their motherland of Armenia. As such, universally, Armenians from all across the world, no matter what province or inhabiting country, identify themselves as Հայ (*Hay*, pronounced "hi").
2 While nowadays Mount Ararat is documented as the highest mountain in Turkey, it was (and to all Armenians is patriotically still) a part of Armenia. The Eastern Anatolia Region in which Mount Ararat is located was considered Armenia's until the Armenian Genocide occurred in 1915, when Turkey overtook that area and from then on claimed the land as its own.
3 In this instance, I refer to Persia's history pre 1 April 1979, before its recognition as the Islamic Republic of Iran. Primarily, I am discussing the classical Persian Empire just prior to the Achaemenid Dynasty.
4 The Bagratid Dynasty refers to the royal dynasty that formally ruled many regional states of Armenia predominantly in the ninth, tenth and eleventh centuries.
5 Van is a city now in an Eastern province of Turkey. At the time of the Armenian Genocide in 1915, the City of Van was under conflict by the Russians and the Young Turks, who both wanted to gain control of the region. It is said that, in 1915, as the killings were beginning, the Armenians staged a rebellion to try to hold onto their city (this was known as the Siege of Van); however, they did not succeed, and by April 1918, Van was under the control of the Ottoman army (Özoğlu, 1996).
6 New Julfa was an area in Persia that was created by Shah Abbas in the seventeenth century, when he relocated an estimated 500,000 Armenians from the north-eastern area of Armenia to a new area of Isfahan, which became known as the Armenian Quarter (Herouni, 2004).
7 By "homeland", I am referring to the English understanding that refers to "one's native land" or "a state, region, or territory that is closely identified with a particular people or ethnic group" (Pearsall & Hanks, 2010).
8 Also known as the security zone, this small strip of land links the Republic of Armenia to Nagorno-Karabakh and the main area, which came under conflict during the Nagorno-Karabakh War.

References

Adalian, R. P. (2015). Armenian Genocide. *Armenian National Institute*. Retrieved from www.armenian-genocide.org/genocide.html

Ahnert, M. A. (2007). *The knock at the door: A journey through the darkness of the Armenian Genocide* (1st ed.). New York: Beaufort Books.

Beck, J. S., & Beck, A. T. (2011). *Cognitive behavior therapy: Basics and beyond* (2nd ed.). New York: The Guildford Press.

Bhabha, H. K. (1992). The world and the home. *Social Text, Third World and Post-Colonial Issues, 31/32*, 141–153.

Bonjukian Patten, C. (2015). Case study: The Armenian Genocide 1915–17. *The Daily Journalist*.

Borger, J. (2019, December 12). US Senate defies Trump in unanimous vote to recognise Armenian Genocide. *The Guardian*, Australia. Retrieved from www.theguardian.com/us-news/2019/dec/12/senate-armenian-genocide-vote-trump-turkey

Chaderjian, P. (2008). Cher the Armenian. *The Armenian Reporter*. Retrieved from www.paulchad.com/2008/02/cher-armenian_1750.html?spref=pi&m=1

Clinton, B. (1994, April 22). *Armenian remembrance day*. Washington, DC: Armenian National Institute.

Cook, A. (2011, Spring). For Hecuba or for Hamlet: Rethinking emotion and empathy in the theatre. *Journal of Dramatic Theory and Criticism*, 71–87.

Cornell, S. E. (1999). *The Nagorno-Karabakh conflict*. Sweden: Uppsala University.

Demytire, R. (2018, May 1). Why Armenia "Velvet Revolution" won without a bullet fired. *BBC News*, Yerevan, Armenia. Retrieved from www.bbc.com/news/world-europe-43948181

Dixon-Johnson, C. F. (1916). *The Armenians*. Northgate, Blackburn: Geo Toulmin & Sons, LTD.

El-Ghusein, F. (1918). *Martyred Armenia*. New York: George H. Doran Company.

European Parliament. (2015). *Armenian Genocide centenary: MEPs urge Turkey and Armenia to normalize relations* [Press release]. Retrieved from http://www.europarl.europa.eu/news/en/news-room/content/20150413IPR41671/html/Armenian-genocide-centenary-MEPs-urge-Turkey-and-Armenia-to-normalize-relations

Gambino, L. (2019, October 30). US house overwhelmingly votes to recognize Armenian Genocide. *The Guardian*, Australia. Retrieved from www.theguardian.com/us-news/2019/oct/29/us-house-overwhelmingly-votes-to-recognize-armenian-genocide

Hegel, G. W. (2003). *The phenomenology of mind* (J. B. Baillie, Trans.). New York: Dover Publications.

Herouni, P. M. (2004). *Armenians and Old Armenia: Archeoastronomy, linguistics, oldest history*. Yerevan, Armenia: Tigran Mets.

Holy Bible: New international version (Vol. King James Version). (1984). New York: Zodervan.

hooks, b. (2009). Kentucky is my fate. In *Belonging: A culture of place*. New York: Routledge.

Hovhannisyan, N., & Mardanyan, S. (2012). *The Armenian Genocide*. Yerevan, Armenia: Zangak Publishing House.

Kevorikian, R. (2011). *The Armenian Genocide: A complete history*. London: I.B. Tauris.

Kifner, J. (2014). Armenian Genocide of 1915: An overview. *The New York Times*. Retrieved from www.nytimes.com/ref/timestopics/topics_armeniangenocide.html

King, C. (2008). *The ghost of freedom: A history of the Caucasus*. New York: Oxford University Press.

Laciner, S. (2008, October 31). Atom Egoyan: Life and his cinema. *The Journal of Turkish Weekly*.

Lazare, A. (2005). *On apology*. Oxford: Oxford University Press.

Lochner, L. P. (1942). *What about Germany?* New York: Dodd, Mead & Company.

Miller, D. E., & Miller, L. T. (1999). *Survivors: An oral history of the Armenian Genocide*. Berkeley, CA: University of California Press.

Narekatsi, G. (1977). *Lamentations of Narek: Mystic soliloquies with god*. London: Mashtots Press.

Nietzsche, F. (1996). *Human, all too human: A book for free spirits* (R. J. Hollingdale, Ed.). London, UK: Cambridge University Press.

Obama commemorates "Meds Yeghern" with statement. (2013, April 24). *The Armenian Weekly*. Retrieved from www.armenianweekly.com/2013/04/24/obama-commemorates-meds-yeghern-with-statement/

Özoğlu, H. (1996). State–Tribe relations: Kurdish tribalism!in the 16th and 17th century Ottoman Empire. *British Journal of Middle Eastern*Studies, 23*(1), 5–27.

Parlakian, N. (2004). *Contemporary Armenian American drama: An anthology of ancestral voices*. New York: Columbia University Press

Payaslian, S. (2007). *The history of Armenia*. London: Palgrave Macmillan.

Pearsall, J. & Hanks, P. (Eds.). (2010). *Oxford dictionary of English* (3rd ed.). London, UK: Oxford University Press.

Persons, J. B. (2008). *The case formulation approach to cognitive-behavior therapy*. New York: The Guilford Press.

Robertson, G. (2009). Was there an Armenian Genocide? Geoffrey Robertson QC's opinion. *Policy Memorandum, Foreign & Commonwealth Office to Minister, 12 April 1999*. Retrieved from www.groong.com/Geoffrey-Robertson-QC-Genocide.pdf

Robertson, G. (2010, October 21) *12:30pm/Interviewer: M. Kenny*. National Press Club Address, ABC News 24, Canberra.

Robertson, G. (2014). *An inconvenient genocide: Who now remembers the Armenians?* North Sydney: Vintage Books by Random House Australia.

Rushdie, S. (1992). *Imaginary homelands, essays and criticism 1981–1991*. London: Granta Books.

Saroyan, W. (1935). The Armenian and the Armenian. In *Inhale and exhale* (pp. 437–438). New York: Random House.

Sassounian, H. (2014, February 11). *Armenian Genocide recognition: Necessary but not sufficiant*. Retrieved from https://www.goggle.com.au/amp/s/www.azatutyun.am/amp/25259716.html

Scammell, R. (2015, April 12). Pope Francis calls Armenian slaughter "genocide". *The Guardian*. Retrieved from www.theguardian.com/world/2015/apr/12/pope-francis- armenian-slaughter-first-genocide-20th-century?CMP=share_btn_fb

Smith, R. W., Markusen, E., & Lifton, R. J. (1995). Professional ethics and the denial of Armenian Genocide. *Holocaust and Genocide Studies, 9*(1), 1–22.

Svazlian, V. (2011). *The Armenian Genocide: Testimonies of the eyewitness survivors*. Yerevan, Armenia: Gitutiun Publishing House.

Torosyan, T. (2012). The origin of the Nagorno Karabakh conflict and its escalation into war. *Slideshare*. Retrieved from www.slideshare.net/Yerevan/the-origin-of-the-nagorno-karabakh-conflict

Ussher, C. D. (1917). *An American physician in Turkey*. Boston, MA and New York: Houghton Mifflin Company.

Waterfield, B. (2015, January 28). Amal Clooney accuses Turkey of hypocrisy on freedom of speech in ECHR Armenian Genocide trial. *The Telegraph*. Retrieved from www.telegraph.co.uk/news/worldnews/europe/turkey/11373991/Amal-Clooney-accuses-Turkey-of-hypocrisy-on-freedom-of-speech-in-Armenian-genocide-trial.html

Wikstrom, C. (2014, October 10). Thousands attend Armenia opposition rally. *Aljazeera*. Retrieved from www.aljazeera.com/news/europe/2014/10/thousands-attend-armenia-opposition-rally-20141010172956457218.html

Էլտայեան, Ն., Հայրապետեան, Մ., & Շահնազարեան, Ն. (1982). *Հայոց Պատմություն: Դասագիրք, տարական դպրոցի և. դասարանի համար*. Թեհրան: Ալիք Տպարան.

4 Dating directing: finding the perfect match

When I grow up I still want to be a director.
(Spielberg, as cited in Corliss, R. 1985, para. 3)

Deconstructing directing

Background

While the history on the emergence of the director's role is uncertain, there were several moments when the director's presence within the theatre took effect. The word "director" is derived from the Greek word *didaskalos*, meaning "teacher". The role took prominence during the nineteenth century; however, the "director" in one form or another has existed since the era of the classical Greeks (Bruch, 1990). Traditionally, Greek theatre or drama began as a religious festival for the gods, of whom the primary one was Dionysus. However, as the festivals became more popular and dramatic competitions began, theatre simply became a part of the culture. Aeschylus, a playwright at the time, began entering many of the dramatic competitions. Eventually, his status grew, and he developed an esteemed reputation. Since then, Aeschylus has often been described as the father of tragedy, as our knowledge of the theatre and drama begins with his work (Cropp, 2005). Although Aeschylus was first and foremost a playwright, his work within the construct of drama holds prominence. Aeschylus, at the time of these festivals, took the existing understanding of "the play" and evolved it through his addition of the second and third actor. By doing so, he not only gave the stories more dramatic variety but also introduced dramatic devices, such as elaborate scenery and dramatic costumes, to help convey the meaning of the narrative. It was fundamentally from there that the playwright-director was unearthed. The playwright not only wrote the plays but also helped to train the chorus musically and dramatically, as well as supervised every other aspect of the production (Brockett & Hildy, 1999). The fact that over time the director became known as *didaskalos* (teacher) is not surprising, as it signifies that, early on, these *directors* amalgamated their roles as author, instructor and "super stage manager" (Cole & Chinoy, 1953, p. 3) in staging their work.

Undoubtedly, the role of the director has advanced and developed since then. The last century, however, has proved pivotal to defining the director's role in more depth. In their book *Directors on Directing – A Source Book of the Modern Theatre*, Toby Cole and Helen-Krich Chinoy (1953) discussed the advancement of the director's role throughout history. They wrote that less than 100 years ago, the director was only an "ideal projected by disgruntled critics of the chaotic Victorian theatre. He [the director] did not even have a name, for the terms 'director', 'regisseur' and 'metteur en scène' had barely begun to acquire their present theatrical meaning" (p. 3). When the director's role finally began to emerge towards the end of the nineteenth century, the function of the director quickly rose in hierarchy over the playwright and actors and became an, if not *the*, authoritative figure. As such, without much hesitation or interval, directors started to mark their individuality and presence on the stage firmly. In line with these thoughts, William Gregory (1968) also investigated the emergence of the director's position within the practice of theatre. He asked, "Who is the director? The director is the final authority and must take full responsibility for any deficiencies in the finished product. He is the person responsible for what the audience sees, hears and feels" (p. 18). Director Robert Benedetti (1985) suggested that in contemporary times, the director acts as an executive and must coordinate the various efforts of the members of this complex organisation towards a specific goal – that is, the production. These authoritative characteristics, to which all the previous authors alluded, resemble what we today recognise as the contemporary director.

Academic texts on the field of directing are still quite rare compared with those concerned with other professions. Susan Cole (1992) believes that one of the major reasons for this is that, unlike most other vocations, directing is still very much a hidden world. The only way to observe directors at work is to be in the rehearsal room with them, and that in itself is an intrusive, rare and delicate undertaking. When I asked directors their thoughts on Cole's opinion, they all in some form agreed and articulated that the elusiveness lies in the fact that directing is a "*hidden art form that happen[s] behind closed doors*" (Metcalf, Interview, 6 March 2014). With this indefinable nature of the profession in mind, to be able to understand completely the nuances and impetus behind the inquiries that I was making into the role, and subsequently into the possible links between directing and identity, the questions that I asked directors began with Gregory's (1968) queries: Who is the director in contemporary theatre today? How does an individual become a director? Why does the individual become a director? What makes a good director?

In Phase 1 of the interviews, I began the sessions with the directors following this logic and Gregory's (1968) and Benedetti's (1985) observations on who the director is in our present day. All the directors interviewed agreed that, currently, the theatre director is the frontrunner, the leader and final decision maker who holds absolute authority over the production and, therefore, needs authoritative qualities to be successful within the role. Director John Kachoyan asserted that "*a good director makes choices, but a great director makes decisions*" (Interview, 28 October 2013). Commended theatre and screen director Aarne Neeme AM echoed Kachoyan's thoughts when saying, "*A director needs to have the qualities of leadership to inspire and bring people together into a unity. This entails a degree of confidence, vision and a genuine response to working with others*" (Interview, 30 August 2013). The directors' responses proved interesting and quite comparable. I agreed with the directors' views and upheld my belief that everyone can call her/himself a director, but not everyone can be notable ones. Subsequently, these responses led me to investigate further the essential qualities of a good director.

Following on from this notion that directing is still an elusive, less-documented vocation compared with other professions, Dr Eric Trumbull (2008), a professor of theatre arts, reported that now that the director is the dominant figure in theatrical production, not only has the interest in theatre directing grown but also suddenly the number of individuals who categorise themselves as directors is increasing. Trumbull's (2008) suggestion fascinated me and seemed to support my understanding that, in current times, anyone can call her/himself a director and few will question this claim. Theatre director Nicholas Hytner alleged, "Most directors become directors by saying 'I'm a director!' and hope someone will believe them" (as cited in Mitchell, 2008, p. 6). As humorous as Hytner's statement is, I agree with him. My observations revealed that individuals can hire a venue and produce a show or make a short film, and instantly, they are at liberty to call themselves directors, and few will challenge the declaration. Esteemed actor, director and playwright Dr Ira Seidenstein asserted his views on the subject:

> *I am very leery of one's motivation and talent for becoming a director. I think a director should come through the ranks so to speak – as an experienced actor or stage manager at least. That is very different than coming in as an "assistant director" without getting one's hands and feet dirty, so to speak.*
> (Interview, 23 August 2013)

Echoing Hytner's and Seidenstein's assessments, I too think that frequently individuals call themselves directors without being challenged. It appears that, unlike many other professions, there are no requisite credentials per se for a director. If this is the case, how does one become (or train to become) a director?

Director Lex Marinos OAM responded,

> *I had no official training in that sense because at that time there weren't a lot of courses doing directing. Even at NIDA [The National Institute of Dramatic Arts] it was about the technical aspect of it, nothing else, so as I got into directing I pieced together the bits from other directors I had observed.*
> (Interview, 16 August 2013)

Similarly, director Joseph Uchitel, at a later interview, said, "*I started my training as a director while I was at acting school. I was extremely lucky to have a teacher who recognised and encouraged my interest. I'm still learning*" (Interview, 2 September 2013). Producer-director Pearl Tan's response was

> *I didn't train to be a director. Initially, I did a Bachelor of Communications majoring in Media Studies and enrolled in a Bachelor of Dramatic Arts*

majoring in Acting. I disliked the theory of drama and instead, I wanted to be able to shape, control and play with the elements of storytelling. It brought together many of my skills and passions, working with actors and other creative people as well as utilising my aptitude for technical things.

(Interview, 6 August 2013)

US/UK playwright-director Bianca Bagatourian simply admitted that she fell into directing and then learnt on the set (i.e. on the job; Interview, 11 September 2013). Therefore, although countless actors pursue formal training, trained directors, in spite of the growing number of institutions offering directing programmes, are relatively uncommon. With this being the case, one has to ask, is the director's role within the context of contemporary theatre, in fact, necessary?

American playwright David Mamet, while primarily identifying himself as a playwright, occasionally adopts the role of director. In his book *Theatre*, Mamet (2010) suggested that the director's role within the theatre is not of primary importance and in fact "can be disposed of" (p. 142). When I was studying at the Atlantic Theater Company Acting School in New York, the actor training was embedded within the teachings of Mamet's work. At the time, I was young and impressionable and engrossed in the technique, so I seldom challenged what I was being taught. Practical Aesthetics is, as it sounds, an action-based practical acting technique that encourages the actor to become self-sufficient and provides the individual with tools to become self-directorial. Although Mamet's comments regarding the disposal of the theatre director are not representative of Practical Aesthetics training, the beginnings of his proposal are acknowledged and at times echoed throughout the school.

As enthusiastic and eager-to-please students at Atlantic, we always endeavoured to create good work for our elite mentors. We worked hard at taking the scripts we were given and directing ourselves within those scenes towards what we considered respectable work. However, as advanced as our scene work was, in my opinion, it did not equate to the requirements of a full production. Although we were creating good work that was appropriate for our peers within the environment of a classroom, I questioned whether we would be able to sustain this type of work ethic for full-length professional productions. Recognising that the role of the director over time has shifted and that its necessity is repeatedly debated, my agreement with Mamet's views on disposal of the director began to sway. Instead, I began to view his proposal as flawed. For his suggestions to be achievable, key rudiments within the process have to be vigilantly thought out. One needs a great script and an experienced group of actors who not only are skilled within their profession but also have awareness across other theatrical elements, such as directing and dramaturgy.

My correspondence with practising directors recurrently revealed that the need for the director to be outside the action was seen as a recognisable feature of the role. Theatre practitioner Gabrielle Metcalf said, "*The director's role is absolutely necessary because it doesn't matter how talented people are they can't look at themselves, or find it very difficult to look at themselves from an audience's perspective*" (Interview, 6 March 2014). Cervonaro articulated this necessity when stating, "*The person that creates the focus of the piece. They [directors] construct the central idea or message and bring to it that third-eye perspective*" (Interview, 23 March 2014). Metcalf's and Cervonaro's comments were only two examples of similar interpretations offered to me by the directors regarding the essential nature of the director's role within the context of theatre. Through these investigations, it became apparent that, besides being the leader, the director's presence within a rehearsal room is arguably advantageous to constructing the overall quality of a production. Because directors are not engrossed in the action of the scene on stage, not only are they able to offer an audience's "third-eye" perspective but also they have the opportunity to assist with any other clarifications that are required regarding crucial moments within the dramaturgy or the scenic composition of the story itself. Echoing Metcalf's thoughts, actors who are immersed in the action of a scene, no matter how talented they may be, find it difficult to recognise gaps within the narrative and offer solutions of linkage of those points in the story. For this reason, I upheld that, at a minimum, the director's role within the process of theatre is needed to offer guidance to the overall implementation of the storytelling process.

Although the evidence strongly pointed towards the director's role being a necessity within the practice and implementation of theatre, these discussions still warranted supplementary examinations into the specifics of the role. To test Mamet's view on the requisite of the director, I used the Kitchen Sink Collective's production of *Yesterday's Hero* (Pike, 2014) as a method of investigation. Watching the results of a directorless production enabled me to reflect on the qualities needed by a director. More importantly, however, *Yesterday's Hero* clarified for me the director's worth to a production.

Collaborative research through the Kitchen Sink Collective

During my time as a doctoral candidate, alongside two fellow researchers, now Dr Gabrielle Metcalf and Dr Shane Pike, I formed a theatre company called the Kitchen Sink Collective. The aim of our company was to take academic research and translate it into mainstream performance. The motivation behind its conception was the need for a forum in which to experiment and investigate some of our methodologies by putting them into practice. Productions during our candidature included *Lifted* (Dobson et al., 2013), *Conversations* (Kitchen Sink Collective, 2014) and *Yesterday's Hero* (Pike, 2014).

In 2013, I attended a rehearsal for *Yesterday's Hero* (Pike, 2014), a play written by Shane Pike. Shane, Gabrielle and I were not able to direct the production because of rehearsal conflicts, so we determined that the play did not need a director and decided to let the actors direct themselves. This decision proved to be a productive experiment for investigating the necessity of the director and why the specific duties that the role encompasses within a production are not a luxury but a requirement.

While watching several rehearsals of *Yesterday's Hero* (Pike, 2014), I contemplated what aspects of the actors' work did not cohere. It was not that their acting was unacceptable or that their commitment to the characters was unmotivated;

instead, it seemed as though there was no direction or "through-line"[1] to the piece. The actors – and in turn their characters – had developed an adequate sense of the work; however, they were so engrossed in the activity of acting that the clarity of the overall story had been compromised. Through my experiences as an actor and director, I knew that key questions, such as *what* story is being told, *whose* story is it and *why* is this story being told, are paramount to the success of an overall production. In *The Shifting Point*, director Peter Brook (1988) described the director's role as comprising two parts: one half, he said, is directing, by which he meant the director is taking charge, making decisions and having the final say; the other half is maintaining the direction or journey of the overall story. Brook described the director as "the one who has studied the map" (p. 6) (i.e. of the play) and becomes a guide, letting everyone know whether they are heading north or south. This lack of clear direction in the Kitchen Sink Collective's production of *Yesterday's Hero* may have affected the overall clarity of the story.

Additionally, through observing rehearsals of *Yesterday's Hero* (Pike, 2014), the question of what qualities make a good director and whether anyone can become a director once again arose. Through this production, I recognised that not everyone can, in fact, be a good director. Recalling Neeme's insights that the role of the director requires an individual with qualities of a leader and visionary (Interview, 20 August 2013), the actors of *Yesterday's Hero*, while talented, seemed to lack the inventiveness and authority required to visually (re)construct an engaging play and do so in an inspiring manner. Whether it was purely their ability at the time of my observations or the possibility that their immersion within their acting roles, as Metcalf understood it, had clouded their ability to perceive the deficiencies, their imaginative ability to see the overall composition of the story and their position as an ensemble was inhibited. This is where I think director's role becomes most profound, as the director is able to observe the action of the scene and guide the actors accordingly towards the imagined objective. When interviewing the directors, I asked what they believed made a good director. Interestingly, comparably to Neeme, all the directors, in some way or another, highlighted the attributes of imagination, leadership and vision. Cervonaro said,

> *I've seen productions where they claimed to be entirely collaborative, but there was lack of cohesion, imagination and a clear dramatic meaning in the piece. With good direction, the audience should walk away with the feeling that they have shared someone's point of view, personality and perceptions about the world around them.*
>
> (Interview, 23 March 2014)

Seidenstein, echoing these thoughts, summed it up as "*a good director can exist in unlimited variations of personality. A good director I think has a unique understanding about people, society, creativity and perhaps theatre. . . . A good director has an honest, informed, and evolving vision of theatre*" (Interview, 23 August 2013). These questions about the attributes or personality traits an individual needs to become a director and the level of proficiency required to execute the role offered interesting areas of study. However, what became most exciting was recognising not only the personality traits needed to become a good director but also *who* chooses to become a director and *why* they choose this authoritative profession.

Turning points in the research

Moment one

Following my discussions with Marinos, Tan and Bagatourian on how one trained to become a director (or rather did not train), I was interested in exploring further the underlying provocations of how one embarks on the profession of directing. Interestingly, few could give me succinct answers. Director Netta Yashchin said,

> *I got into directing upon arriving to Australia. With a thick Hebrew accent and a lot of experience as an actor I started leading workshops and sharing my knowledge. At first it was sheer practicality, but later on I discovered it was something I found out I could do and do well.*
>
> (Interview, 10 December 2013)

Neeme replied,

> *For me the interest was in working together with others to create a "World" that then was shared with an audience. As an "outsider" and being painfully shy outside my cultural community, it was a means of building a controlled situation and dealing with others. A sublimation of the need to belong and communicate. The cultural background of my father being an artist, and my mother having grown up in a theatre that was managed by her parents, surely played a part as well.*
>
> (Interview, 20 August 2013)

Correspondingly, Marinos noted,

> *Really, at the end of the day, directing gave me better control for my opinion. During the playwright's conference in the 1970s, this was a breeding ground for new writers. At the ANU Conference, really the climate and timing had a lot to do with it. I was suddenly given these plays and people would say "Here, why don't you direct this". It found its way towards me and I found my way towards it I guess. . . . Directing provided me with a fresh challenge and it was something I wanted to start doing. The identity I had through acting was very limiting and directing gave me better control.*
>
> (Interview, 20 August 2013)

After hearing comparable considerations from several others, I was able to recognise an element of directing that was well known to me: that an individual who gravitates towards directing is a storyteller who has the ability to see beyond the text. This individual generally demonstrates leadership attributes, has the ability to see the overall objective of a story and has an imagination that leads to a *vision* of the overall production. What I had initially considered *my* distinctive transition into the profession of directing proved not so unique. It appeared that many directors had also transitioned into the profession via another creative career.

The decision to pursue directing commonly arose from involvement with another creative art form, such as acting or writing. Further, becoming a director seemed to take place via three varied routes: direct choice, accidently and forcedly. The majority of the directors interviewed had no formal training but rather had created their unique directing styles by adapting what they had learnt through their work as actors or through the observations they made of the directors with whom they had worked. French-Australian director Jean-Pierre Mignon observed,

> *I didn't train to be a director. In the drama course I attended in Paris, which was affiliated to a theatre company, I was given the opportunity to direct fellow students and then further my training, if you like, by becoming the assistant director to the company director.*
>
> (Interview, 14 September 2013)

Marinos replied, "*I guess I pieced together the bits from other directors. Nothing official in that sense. I put into practice what I learned about other directors*" (Interview, 16 August 2013). Marinos's reply was almost identical to that of Neeme, who said, "*I learnt mostly by doing, but also through watching others' [directors'] processes and products*" (Interview, 20 August 2013). Seidenstein also commented that he had become a director through his work as an actor and clown. "*I heard actors critiquing/criticising the main director. Coinciding with a 'discovering' of clowning I thought clowning could be a way to discover what a director goes through in terms of overall responsibility for the creation of a performance*" (Interview, 23 August 2013). Seidenstein's remarks also supported qualities of leadership as he continued to explain that through the requests of his colleagues, he coincidently found himself at times directing and acting concurrently. However, Seidenstein outlined that he learnt how to be a director fundamentally through working with other highly experienced directors and later in his career developed his craft further via his own methodology of Core Mechanics – a short movement kata (choreographed patterns of movements) that he created, which also happened to hold the keys to learning how to control the actor's body in space. This gave him the insights into the director's responsibility of blocking (classical stage direction) or mise en scéne (Interview, 23 August 2013). I began to wonder if, as acknowledged by these directors, individuals commonly evolve or advance into the director's role via another means – that is, by learning "on the job", per se, via trial and error. Then why do individuals make that transition into directing (or feel the need to), and what is it about the vocation that draws them in?

Moment two

During the early stages of my research, my primary aim was to take the core fundamentals of Practical Aesthetics (Bruder et al., 1986) that were developed by Mamet and see if they could be interpolated into a directing process for new contemporary directors and students working with naturalistic, text-based plays. The research stemmed from my understanding that aspiring directors, at times, become so concerned with the overall vision of their plays that the communication of the playwrights' intentions becomes lost in the process. By observing emerging directors, I recognised that, at times, they find it hard to understand that there is more to directing a play than simply their vision. Additionally, many young directors find it difficult to communicate their ideas to the actors and thereby fail to realise their overall concepts concerning the text and its interpretation. If aspiring directors knew a practical and simple way of tackling the analysis and understanding the script, then they would be able to go into the rehearsal room with a comprehensive understanding of the play and thus communicate their ideas clearly to the actors. Practical Aesthetics, as one of the few contemporary acting techniques that is writer driven, offered the perfect testing model to support my initial idea that once an aspiring director has conducted the "groundwork" on a script and understands how to tackle the analysis of the text clearly, s/he can confidently go forth and implement her/his vision of the overall play, starting with the crucial task of blocking the actors. My intention of using the Practical Aesthetics script analysis method was founded on the idea that, like the actors who studied the technique, if directors can gain the tools to identify a clear idea of what the play is about and how it is constructed, then s/he can work with the team in a coherent manner and guide the rehearsal room into a productive state.

However, after much trial and error, I realised that while the compilation of a practical handbook for the director might still be useful within the industry, the focus on a rigid and structured acting technique such as Practical Aesthetics and interpolation of that system into a standard directing technique would produce major obstacles. First, while Practical Aesthetics is a productive form of actor training, it presents many limitations when adapted into a technique for directors. Unlike actors, who need to be able to deconstruct aspects of their characters and investigate all parts pertaining to them prior to entering a rehearsal, directors devote much more time to scriptural and thematic research and can only analyse and imagine a script to some degree before needing the work or ideas and imaginations of the actors within a rehearsal room. Second, I began to accept that directing is a subjective art form. Directors do not tend to share the same vision when interpreting a script, and they do not employ only one method or style of directing. I became curious about the many methods or processes involved in directing. During observations, some techniques I encountered were not necessarily ones with which I agreed as a director, but nonetheless, I appreciated the assortment of ideas to which an emerging director could have access.

In Chapter 1, "Attracted to Theatre: Setting the Scene", I discussed the possible reasons why individuals might be drawn to the *theatre* and why they may find solace within its construct. I briefly questioned what might have attracted me to the art form, but now I was interested in specifically looking at the position of the director within this paradigm. Through the aforementioned dialogue, I sketchily determined what the role of the director encompasses and what qualities are needed. Past directors have articulated that they did not necessarily choose the role but rather it chose them, with many communicating that it was almost a compulsion that drew them into the role. Where did this compulsion come from? Directing greats Brecht (1977), Stanislavski (1962) and Artaud (1958) all led troubled lives and struggled with their own sense of identity and belonging, giving up promising careers in politics, medicine and writing to pursue creative paths as directors (Roose-Evans, 1970). I began to ask, are there personal motivations or key initiatives that lead individuals into pursuing directing? Could the attraction to the role possibly have something to do with the notion that, as directors, individuals know where their standing is within the theatre community and, while absorbed in the activity of directing, s/he struggles less frequently with this concept of self? Further, what if it is not the work itself that the director finds compelling but some other incentive? Maybe the reasoning revolves around the exploration of directors' identities as leaders, visionaries, recreators and storytellers within the work they direct that gives them a sense of purpose in their lives? I initiated this exploration by first looking at my particular inauguration into the role.

To be or not to be

It was a trying time attempting to forge some sort of career in the performing arts as a culturally different young individual in the early 2000s. In Australia, although opportunities were growing, there were very few roles available to multicultural actors straight out of drama school, and the few available seemed to go to the most experienced of the group. I felt that, as an actor, I was not in charge of my future. When, finally, diversity seemed to blossom within the industry, stereotyping of multicultural ethnicities, unfortunately, seemed to follow. Marinos remembers that the identity he had as an actor was very limiting:

> *You know we were put into a box, Greeks, Italians, Lebanese it really didn't matter, you were genetically foreign so you can play them. I remember thinking, this is crazy, it's not representative of who we are and really I had nothing more to bring to it. It was very limiting. Directing, however, gave me better control of my opinion.*
>
> (Interview, 16 August 2013)

Marinos's understandings resonated with my experiences growing up, as I too felt forever culturally stereotyped and displaced. I was not Armenian but I did not feel Australian either. I was stuck somewhere in between the worlds, and this "to-ing and fro-ing" carried through into my identity as an actor. I did not look like the stereotypical Australian female, but I did not sound ethnic either. I remember going to see an agent who said, "I really like you but I have no idea where to put you on my books", meaning he was not sure which box to file me under – Mediterranean, Middle Eastern, Australian or other. I was not surprised. I did not know what box to file myself under either. I too was going through an "identity crisis", and I was not sure if I was Persian-Armenian, Armenian, Armenian-Australian, Australian or something else.

As discussed in Chapter 2, "Seeking Identity: Searching for Self", following Erikson's (1963a) and Schultz and Schultz's (2008) views on "identity crisis", I consider that the rise of the "identity crisis" and, thereafter, the resolutions of these conflicts happen differently for each individual. Through observation of my family and friends, I have found that some deal with their conflicts by travelling; others by painting, writing, renovating or divorcing; and others turn to crime or illegal substances. Schultz and Schultz (2008) called the latter of these suggestions a "negative identity" (p. 169). I, in contrast, dyed my hair, believing somehow that going blonde and looking "more Australian" would provide clarity to my struggles. It did not. Neither did going burgundy, bright red or chestnut, for that matter. What did help, however, was my love for the theatre as I slowly began to work through this period of adolescence. Erikson (1963b) advised that this "adolescent period" takes place between the ages of 18 and 40 and is *the* most crucial stage for the development of people's identities in setting up the rest of their lives. By the end of this period, I was confidently transitioning into adulthood and simultaneously had made the passage into my new role as a director. My focus had now turned away from my inequalities to focus on the creative developments of my projects within the theatre and my position as a leader.

Theatre director Anne Bogart (2001) wrote, "Directing chose me as much as I chose it. We found one another" (p. 1). Like Bogart, as I made my transition from actor to director, alleviation of some kind enveloped me. My cultural differences slowly began to diminish and, as a result, the probing questions surrounding my ethnicity began to disperse. What remained was Soseh the storyteller. It seemed that directing allowed me an autonomy I had never felt as an actor – a freedom to take a play, interpret it and envision it the way I thought the story should be told. Instead of separating and running away from who I was, through my work as a theatre director, I was able to take the pages of a play and saturate them with my uniqueness. It appeared that, through directing, I had managed to find some sense of belonging that up until that point in my life I had never felt. The "identity crisis" that had plagued me for such a long time was slowly waning and, not long after these "resolutions" (Erikson, 1963a), I returned my hair colour to its original black.

Reflection on these events in my life uncovered an aspect of directing that was not commonly articulated. Could the link between a culturally displaced individual finding an authoritative voice and a sense of purpose (and, in turn, self) through the vocation of directing be where the appeal lay? Cervonaro considered that "*directing provides the individual a platform to voice their point of view, to share their stories in ways they see as important, and to collaborate with others towards this common goal*" (Interview, 23 March 2014). Bagatourian responded,

Directing definitely gives you a sense of belonging. I think any individual in the creative field is on a simultaneous track of finding themselves. Every time we create, we are giving birth to a small part of ourselves, which in turn helps us to know ourselves better.

(Interview, 11 September 2013)

As did Neeme, who said,

Many an individual who has struggled with their identity has found solace and release through art forms. Directing definitely provides you with a sense of belonging. The company you work in and the people you reach, are really a microcosm of the wider community. There is a joke, that any township with more than a dozen inhabitants will form a drama group!

(Interview, 20 August 2013)

Kachoyan considered,

Yes, but only if they [the individual] wants to explore their own sense of identity. Directing gives you a voice and with a voice you can speak up and say whatever you want about anything. A voice represents who you are so directing is a way to express yourself and share your experience.

(Interview, 28 October 2013)

Admired theatre director Anthony Skuse insisted that for him, directing was about agency:

I got into directing because I think I felt I had a broader view of the kind of work I wanted to make. I felt as an actor I didn't have enough control of the other elements. I used to see decisions being made and think why are you doing that. For me it was about being a painter with a palette and being able to apply the colours and apply them how I saw fit.

(Interview, 16 February 2014)

Through these interviews, I began to appreciate that the links between directing and identity could now bear fruit. In the following subsections, I will expand on the interviews that were conducted with the directors and what areas of inquiry I concentrated on and why.

Homing versus belonging

Phase 1 of the interviews focused on uncovering the links between directing and identity. I asked the directors indirectly and then, towards the latter stages of the interview, directly, "Do you believe an individual who has been culturally displaced and *unhomed* can find identity and a sense of belonging through directing?" Careful examination of their answers revealed that directing does, in fact, assist an individual in finding a sense of belonging, but how this is achieved is what proved interesting. The research revealed that the majority of directors do not have a hard time leaving behind a production. Commonly, actors experience difficulties letting go of a play and their characters. However, for directors, as soon as opening night arrives, it is as if they have been relieved of their post and handed over ownership of the production to the cast and crew. As a result, directors can then begin to work on a new project, if they have not already done so. Skuse replied that, for him, directing is a continuous journey that starts and keeps going: "*Even when it ends a new one starts again*" (Interview, 16 February 2014). Director Sam Cleary said he never had a hard time letting go of a production. In fact, at times, he works on several projects at once (Interview, 15 March 2014). Skuse's and Cleary's reflections were not uncommon. It seemed that several of the directors shared this perspective. This natural progression for a director is analogous to that of a spiral. The director begins a process of directing with a group of actors; develops a unique bond, forming a kind of community; and then once the production or play has opened and the rehearsal process has come to an end, the director abandons that specific group and moves on to begin the process all over again with a new group. Interestingly, Metcalf's comments favoured this transience in the profession:

> *It's a collaboration of this little nucleus where you're all creating this one thing and then it's gone. I think the transient nature of it is so unique. It's in that moment where you create that thing. We have these four weeks to create something and then it's gone.*
>
> (Interview, 6 March 2014)

Similarly, director Steven Truscott described that:

> *Every time I begin a new project it's a new script, new group of actors, creatives, everything is a start all over process. There are things I carry into each new show but for the most part it's all new and we have to start from scratch. I love that about the profession.*
>
> (Interview, 18 March 2014)

It fascinated me that directing, and theatre more generally, can speak to this sense of dislocation and that through the performing arts, an individual can find a sense of *home*. It appeared that the individual, by the very choice of becoming a director, further *unhomed* her/himself because of the nature of directing. Although they feel a sense of home within a group for a period, it is only a matter of time before an upheaval takes place, and they once again find themselves unsettled. This means that the sense of belonging is attained because directing allows the individual to have a sense of purpose, experience achievement and, in turn, develop a sense of identity through the work. Through reflection on his own theatre productions as a director, Skuse observed that the sense of belonging for him is found in the sentiment of family that forms in the group, depending on the play they are working on. He said, "*You find creatives[2] you like to work with, actors who you end up sharing* a history with and sometimes depending on the play, you share an experience both creatively and personally which is unique and life changing" (Interview, 16 February 2014). Echoing Skuse's thoughts, Cervonaro said,

> *For many directors, particularly theatre directors, the process is not solitary and often, for both cast and crew, a sense of belonging to a family develops when they begin working on a particular story. When an individual has this clear purpose and direction in their work, inevitably it creates a strong sense of identity.*
> (Interview, 23 March 2014)

Director Anthony Yarra noted that the collaboration gives the individual a sense of belonging. He said that, in directing, even more so than in any other profession, the director is the leader and, as such, "*you have a purpose, responsibility, everyone is looking up to you and you know where your place is*" (Interview, 27 March 2014). With a clarity about the role and where that role is positioned within the hierarchy of a rehearsal room, culturally displaced individuals can easily find a sense of purposefulness through the practice of directing but, more importantly, within the context of the theatre, s/he can find a perception of "home" – a familiar ground where they are at ease, relaxed and comfortable (Pearsall & Hanks, 2010).

In line with Chapter 2's discussions on the complexities and multiplicities of *home*, Zandy reminds us that "home is an idea, an inner geography where the ache to belong finally quits, where there is no sense of 'otherness', where there is at last, a community" (as cited in Friedman, 2004, p. 195). Interpreting Zandy's idea of home as a place of comfort, ease and space free of otherness, it appeared home in the context of theatre directing is not found within the activity of directing, as I had initially thought. Instead, the theatre as a communal space void of difference becomes the home, and belonging is found through the operational aspects with the others in the room. Further, the directors' comments seemed to be alluding to the idea that this notion or illusion of belonging does not actually lie solely in the final production, which I had assumed was the case. Instead, the sense of belonging is found through the action of directing – that is, the *journey* that the director takes in the (re)construction of a production. If directing is then a spiral of infinite creation, maybe the answers surrounding belonging and identity warranted further investigation.

Phase 1 confirmed that the possible links between directing and identity were plausible, and this was connected, for the most part, to the director's sense of purpose in the role of leader. That is to say, although s/he may lack clear direction or bearing within her/his own life, in the theatre and specifically within her/his responsibility as a director, s/he adopts the persona of chief and thus creatively has a clear focus on where s/he belongs within the framework of the theatre. Indeed, Cleary said,

> *For me it comes back to this idea of being needed. As the director I am needed for something and it [the show] can't be done without me. Well that's enough to make anyone feel like they belong, especially if they haven't ever felt that through their life.*
> (Interview, 15 March 2014)

78 *Dating directing*

Prior to this research, I had assumed that directors find their sense of self within the work they choose to produce, within the stories, where they are able to recreate an imaginary world unique to them that is saturated with their individuality. However, the more I questioned this with the directors, the more I came to understand that although this sense of self is reflected in the director's work, fundamentally, the sense of belonging exists within the director's process or activity of directing and within the collaborative family-like culture that exists. "Home", therefore, seems to exist within the framework of the theatre itself and, therefore, directing, being an *unhoming* profession, does not complicate the matter. In my mind, I began to sketch how this infinite spiral-like process might look. Figure 4.1 is a depiction of this sketch.

If my hunch held some truth and the idea of a *home* (D) is found within the construct of the *theatre*, and A (the individual) finds C (belonging) through B (the action of directing) via this infinite process of creation, then what is so unique about this *journey*? Do the answers lie in the stories that the directors choose to tell and how they choose to portray them, or is it the communal aspect of the journey and not the work at all? If, as theatre director Gale Edwards once suggested, directing is an

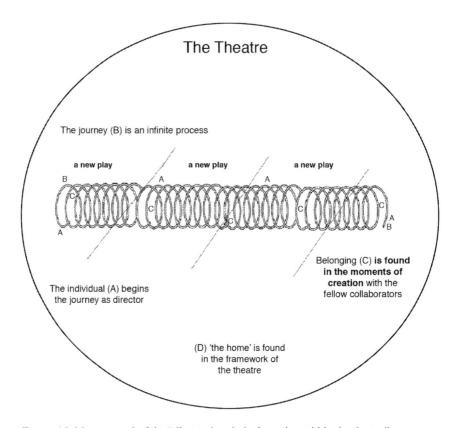

Figure 4.1 My portrayal of the "director's spiral of creation within the theatre"

unpredictable and at times experimental vocation that "warranted itself to isolation and criticism" (as cited in Ward, 1988, p. 11), then why do individuals choose it? Maybe the answers lay in the creative elements of the profession. To gain a deeper understanding of the impetus behind an individual transitioning into the authoritative profession and to investigate how these were linked to this idea of the *journey*, a new broader range of directors needed to be interviewed and new questions had to be formulated. These motivations led me to Phase 2 of the interviewing process.

The director's journey

Phase 2 of the interviews set out to discover more detail about the directors' perceptions of their profession. Phase 2 consisted of questions such as the following:

- What do you think are some of the unique qualities that directing provides an individual that no other creative field will allow a person to do?
- It is often said that you don't choose directing but instead it (the profession) chooses you; what do you think about this statement?
- Do you believe a director's role is necessary, and if so, why?

While the responses from the directors were varied, surprisingly, they commonly described the uniqueness of this journey with a sense of affection towards fellow collaborators. Therefore, they were focusing not simply on the work but also on the people with whom they created the work. Many of the directors used terms such as community, shared experience, creativity, collaboration and family. Tan observed,

> *I like that it [directing] brings together many of my skills at the same time and within a group. I strive to be good at working with other people, with technical things, with creative things. Creativity has shown me that you need to let go and just enjoy the journey, as corny as that sounds.*
> (Interview, 6 August 2013)

Skuse reflected,

> *It's the collaboration and working with people . . . the depth of the relationships you create with your actors, or the type of relationship is extraordinary, I don't know if you find that intimacy and openness in any other profession.*
> (Interview, 16 February 2014)

Director-producer Stephanie Glover similarly noted the intimate nature of the profession, articulating that "*it's the people and the sharing of stories and sometimes intimate stories at that. There's a trust that develops within the sacredness of the space that ultimately leads to a sense of admiration, purpose and belonging*" (Interview, 2 April 2014). Throughout the various responses, the uniformity of the emphasis placed on social interaction within a group or family-like environment was remarkable. It indicated to me why, potentially, a culturally displaced individual might actually find a sense of belonging through the activity of directing.

Being in a rehearsal room over an extended period of time and working closely with a group of actors sometimes forces you to share personal insights into your individual identity, which you may not need to do otherwise. Usually, some sort of recognition of a likeness between life experience and the characters' predicament activates these insights into the play's narrative. Just as a director will ask actors to reflect on their own lives to find parallels with the lives of their characters, actors often ask the same from their director. The unity that this intimate process creates within the rehearsal room is very like that of a family. It produces an atmosphere of protection, friendship and affection, which can not only be addictive but also therapeutic. Skuse's sentiments were as follows:

> *I mean you find a family in the theatre don't you. You find creatives you like to work with. Actors who you end up sharing a history with and sometimes, depending on the play, you share an experience both creatively and personally which is unique and life changing and rarely found anywhere else.*
> (Interview, 16 February 2014)

I began to consider my own experiences in light of his thoughts and the thoughts of the other directors I had interviewed, and I realised that my personal familiarity as a displaced adolescent may have found consolation in the impressions of family that the theatre provided.

In his book *Working Together in Theatre: Collaboration and Leadership*, Robert Cohen (2011) wrote a great deal about this idea of theatre repeatedly being referred to as a family. Although he used many variations of this concept, such as ensemble family, backstage family, virtual family, artistic family, pseudo family and family of strangers, Cohen suggested that, at its most primitive level, this illusion of family dates back to when theatre companies and the circus were first created and were, at their core, family businesses. He added that, while blood-linked theatre companies are extremely rare today, the traditions of it remain. Cohen then further discussed the director's role within this so-called *family* by asserting that directing requires "skills that reach into the emotional hearts and unconscious minds of those being directed. And it should not be surprising, when collaborating theatre artists consider themselves as a family, that they consider their director as a parent" (p. 56). While many of the directors I interviewed articulated this notion of family in a positive manner – that is, one that generates an environment of protection, friendship and warmth – it is important to note that, among these delights, as Cohen warned, this idea of family within the theatre is not without quarrels. Like most families, there are also the "misunderstandings, emotional conflicts, sibling rivalries, temper tantrums, parental resentments and longstanding hierarchies handed down through generations" (p. 193).

By this phase of the research, I had begun to assemble the puzzle. If the appreciation of *home* is found within the framework of the theatre, *family* is found with the collaborators and *belonging* is found through the activity of directing and the people, then how does the sense of identity form? How does the link between the individual as a person and the individual as director take shape? Does it now go beyond the space of the theatre and the cast and creatives and move towards the text of the play? If so, how is this connection formed? Maybe this journey is a mutation of the activity of directing and the stories or plays a director chooses to tell. Several of the directors identified that the journey is a combination of the activity of directing and the role. At times, many could not even separate the two thoughts. What if, contrary to what I had originally supposed, my sense of identity is not *only* experienced through the stories that I choose to direct but also accessed through another aspect of the text?

Through the comments from the directors interviewed, I now accepted that this concept of family, purpose, belonging, authority and the *journey* are credible facets that play vital roles within this area of exploration. However, I was still committed to determining whether the work created by directors (i.e. the stories they choose to tell or the text) also plays an important part. That is why, through directing *No Worries* (Holman, 1989) and *Uncle Jack* (Lonnie, 2014), I set out to explore in what ways the chosen plays contributed towards this director's journey. Were the aspects of identity and/or individuality reflected throughout the similarities of these productions, which possibly mirrored both the director's identity and the individuals? Did the elements of identity have any corresponding links to the actual script or story, or could a sense of self be found via another process, through the differences maybe? Further, how did these distinctions filter through to the methods that were employed by the director, either in the rehearsal room or throughout the production?

Immersion into the practice of directing

No Worries *and* Uncle Jack

Background

Throughout my career, I have often found myself directing plays that deal with themes with which I am familiar in my personal life, such as racism, dissimulation, isolation, displacement, cultural matters and bullying. Whether I choose them deliberately or otherwise, these themes seem to be the core issues that attract me as a director. On this topic, Mignon remarked, "*Similarly, I am interested in plays that challenge an audience, plays that help us understand life and ourselves better*" (Interview, 14 September 2013). Seidenstein stated, "*I think my cultural drive is on two levels and it definitely informs my personal motivation in acting as a director*" (Interview, 23 August 2013). Comparably, Marinos determined that, due to his experiences, he "*wanted scripts that broke down the stereotypes because of my experiences as an actor. I wanted to break down the stereotypes and really do work on a purely human level*" (Interview, 16 August 2013). Through these responses, I began to recognise that directors are drawn to specific types of work or influences that they identify with as individuals or at least work that provokes personal emotional responses. However, my involvement in *No Worries* and *Uncle Jack* was particularly thought provoking because, for the first time in my career, I was directing two plays and, as a director, connecting with their overarching narratives and representations of stereotypical Australia, but doing so in a skewed way and possibly not how the playwrights had intended.

No Worries is a Theatre in Education (TIE) play written by English playwright David Holman. Over time, the play has become recognisable as an iconic Australian story. At the heart of the story are the trials and tribulations of a 10-year-old girl named Matilda. Matilda's life is completely turned upside down when her parents are forced to move to the city because of an extensive period of drought. The story then proceeds to explore core themes of isolation, dissimulation, bullying and racism as we follow Matilda and her family's struggles in adjusting to their new lives. *Uncle Jack*, in contrast, is a contemporary play written by Perth playwright Ross Lonnie. Lonnie combines lyrical, poetic stories of war and tales of Anzac bravery in an autobiographical account of the toll that war took on its Australian veterans, specifically exploring the after-effects of post-traumatic stress disorder (PTSD).

As a director, my relationship to these stories proved interesting. With *No Worries*, while I had empathy for the play's various themes of bullying and racism, I was not, like the character at the core of the story, a first-generation Australian country girl raised in the hardships of the Australian outback. Nor did I have any first-hand knowledge of what it is like to live in rural Australia where drought plagues everyday existence. Therefore, although I was familiar with the various themes that the story presented, Holman's representation of stereotypical rural Australia and his own familiarities with Australians were far removed from my first-hand accounts. Indeed, I often found Holman's depiction of Australia, Australians and the character of the recently arrived Vietnamese refugee Binh naïve and, at times, insulting. Similarly, this view also transitioned into my initial reactions towards *Uncle Jack*. As an Armenian, I relate to the anniversary of the Anzacs differently. To me, the day embodies the beginnings of Armenia's devastating 1915 genocide. While there is no doubt about my empathy for what Australia's war veterans endured, I resent the lack of recognition of the fact that, on the same day Australia was fighting with the Ottoman Empire in Gallipoli, the Ottoman Empire was slaughtering over one-and-a-half million Armenians in towns and villages very close to Gallipoli, in Cilicia. My resentment was enhanced, in part, by the timing of *Uncle Jack*. It was produced to commemorate the centenary of Gallipoli, concurrent with the centenary of the Armenian Genocide.

My experience directing the two plays, therefore, raised two vital questions. First, I wondered if a director's sense of identity throughout "the journey" is not necessarily found only through identifying with the play or story but can also be unearthed through the differences or the undesirable emotions that it raises. This overturned an important understanding in my ideology as a director, as prior to directing Holman's *No Worries* and Lonnie's *Uncle Jack*, I may have rejected the idea of directing plays on this subject matter. Instead, I accepted my aversions to the stereotypical depictions of Australia that both stories raised and my contrary reactions towards Anzac Day, which *Uncle Jack* explored. As a director, by permitting myself to go on a journey and through the differences potentially find the similarities, suddenly, both stories' superficial elements were transcended. In their place, the themes of bullying and the devastation wreaked by conflicts of war were clarified, arousing in me new appreciations as a director. Second, I began to wonder whether there might be value in directors taking on plays with content outside their areas of knowledge or stories that aroused different understandings in them towards the play.

Stereotype, defamiliarisation and difference

Growing up in the western suburbs of Sydney within a traditionally Armenian environment meant that the majority of information I had in relation to Australian culture was largely filtered through iconic Australian television shows, such as *Neighbours* (Various, 1985–present) and *Home and Away* (Various, 1988–present). Besides the six to eight hours a day I spent at school, and considering that the small group of friends I had were mostly Mediterranean, the only access I had to "Australia" was through official and often paradoxical representations of its people and culture. In fact, I did not have a real "Australian" friend until I reached primary school, and even then, I remember thinking how different looking she was from me. The way her skin looked, her dress sense, where and how she lived, the food she ate, the topics of conversation she would discuss were all so different from mine. My parents often articulated the distinctions between my Armenian friends and my Australian friends, signifying immediate divisions. During the productions of *No Worries* and *Uncle Jack*, these insights became significant, as prior to my research, I had firmly believed that directors can and, moreover, should only direct plays with stories that resonate with them through first-hand familiarities with the narrative. I often found myself affronted when I saw plays written about migrants or cultural displacement that were directed by Anglo-Saxons, who, I assumed at the time, had no direct connection to the stories' themes. I thought that unless directors personally understood the topics being presented in the story, there was no way s/he could direct the play with the integrity and consideration the piece deserves.

Twentieth-century Russian theorist and literary critic Viktor Shklovsky (1917) had alternate views on this matter. Shklovsky postulated that if individuals see an *object* so often that it becomes familiar to them, those objects lose their meaning and instead become recognised automatically, without much thought or influence. He determined that a form of habitualisation takes effect and instead such objects lead to a kind of blind spot in the individual's observation. Therefore, the object's true weight and full materialistic or symbolic sense lose its effect. Shklovsky suggested that to see an object truly in the fullness of its meaning, that object needs to be defamiliarised[3] or made strange to once again have its full desired influence. Although he attributed the processes of defamiliarisation predominantly to language, he also commented on it in reference to art, declaring,

> The purpose of art is to impart the sensation of things as they are perceived and not as they are known. The technique of art is to make objects "unfamiliar", to make forms difficult, to increase the difficulty and length of perception because the process of perception is an aesthetic end in itself and must be

84 *Dating directing*

prolonged. Art is a way of experiencing the artfulness of an object; the object is not important.

(Shklovsky, 1917, p. 778)

Although Shklovsky discussed "art" here within the literary sense of poems and prose, I argue that the characteristics that the literary world adopts, such as plot, setting, character and language, can also be found within the theatrical world and in particular in the activity of directing. Shklovsky's (1917) concepts of defamiliarisation strengthened my work as a director in *No Worries* and *Uncle Jack*.

As a director, I approached the direction of both plays by asking myself questions as I always do: (1) what are my passions and appreciations of these stories and (2) why do audiences need to see it today? While the process of answering these questions was not straightforward, generally, once I began to do so, gradually, the pieces began to connect and so did my allegiance to the stories. As a playwright-driven director, I search for answers within a script by investigating *what* the story is about, *how* the playwright is telling it (i.e. the literary conventions being used and the perspective of the narrative) and *why* s/he is telling it. I then explore the key themes and overall through-line of the story, and once an understanding is established around that, I decide not only what the significance of that message is but also in what way I as the director want the audience to receive that message. For example, is the message's tone positive or negative and what (if any) is the social commentary of the work? Once I have gained some form of understanding of these questions, I am able to begin applying my overall vision to the piece, leading the cast and creatives to the eventual objective: the production of the play.

Both Holman's *No Worries* and Lonnie's *Uncle Jack*, in their own unique ways, represent iconic Australian stories. When I was reading the plays, it was difficult to ignore the Australian clichés throughout both stories. For example, Holman's play commences with the iconic Australian folk songs "Waltzing Matilda" and "Road to Gundagai", followed by introductions to a few of its key characters. The protagonist, aptly named Matilda Bell, likewise reprises iconic Australian lines, such as "she'll be right, Dad" and "no worries, mate!" (Holman, 1989). Similarly, Lonnie's play opens with the character of Uncle Jack singing the Australian folk song "It's a Long Way to the Riverina" while drinking a longneck[4] before the character of Doug enters, clothed in a full Australian army officer's uniform. In their own ways, both casts in rehearsals found Holman's and Lonnie's representations of Australia and the literary devices used patronising and almost satirical, as did I at times, but in an altered way. For the cast, the depictions were insulting and many remarked, "Australians don't talk like that and we don't wear that type of clothing". It was for that reason that the actors in both instances wanted to *play down* the Australian clichés as much as possible. I, however, found Holman's and Lonnie's depictions of Australians humorous, as they immediately made me think how stereotypically "Aussie" and unsubtle these choices were. Moreover, they were not too far a stretch from the images that I grew up with on my television screen or my familiarities with cultural stereotyping. Therefore, because of my pre-existing ideas of Australia, I had plans to exaggerate these distinctive qualities as far as realistically conceivable. I knew that to make the issues within the story and the poignancy of the characters stand out and become serious points of discussion, instead of shying away from the parodies of "Australiana", as a director, I had to reproduce them with overstated features as much as was believably possible. This raises an interesting argument: how can something be truthful if it is stereotypical, which commonly means a representation that reduces so-called common characteristics to a kind of shorthand based simply on bias?

Professor Chinua Achebe once said, "The whole idea of a stereotype is to simplify. Instead of going through the problem of all this great diversity – that it's this or maybe that – you have just one large statement; it is this" (as cited in Blount-Nuss, 2011, p. 8). While the majority of the scholarly resources follow Achebe and determine that stereotyping is negative and reduces the individual, researchers have continually asked whether there is a kernel of truth behind stereotyping. In *Stereotypes, Cognition and Culture*, Dr Perry Hinton (2000) debated this idea of truth and stereotype. Primarily, he argued that stereotyping is related to prejudice and has many faults. However, I found Hinton's interpretation of the ideas of Walter Lippmann (1922) and Gordon Allport (1954) particularly interesting. Both Lippmann and Allport implied that there are cognitive approaches to understanding the impulses behind stereotyping. They advocate that although stereotyping may seem to be simplistic, it is not. The need for it arose out of the processes of common understanding and awareness. As human beings, we need to categorise the social world to understand and interact with it and, thus, we use stereotyping as a convention to do so. Lippmann and Allport suggest these are not mental failings but rather features of the way human cognition operates (as cited in Hinton, 2000). For that reason, while exaggerated, Holman's and Lonnie's representations of Australia were to a degree no different from mine. Even though the scripts do not depict the Australia of today (although that too is debatable), they engraved in my mind a truthful or one might say comforting portrayal of the stereotype of nostalgic, mythological Australia, which quite possibly is still imprinted in the mind of the audience.

Whether it was because of my instincts as a migrant Australian or my tacit understanding of storytelling as a director, I inherently used Shklovsky's (1917) ideas of defamiliarisation in my direction of *No Worries* and *Uncle Jack*. It began on a subconscious level, and then I deliberately focused on emphasising the plays' stereotypical portrayals of Australia (characters, set, costumes, language and behaviour). By doing so, I was able to bring significance to moments within the plays that otherwise might have been overlooked. For instance, in *No Worries*, I made deliberate decisions that were not within Holman's script. I emphasised the idea of Australiana by adopting such tropes as using an outback caravan on a bed of red dirt for the set (see Figure 4.2); dressing the actors in clichéd KingGee shorts, wife-beater singlets, flannelette shirts and R. M. Williams work boots; and asking the narrator to wear a hat with dangling bottle corks, as depicted in the character sketches (see Figure 4.3). All of these choices played towards Shklovsky's (1917) ideas of exaggeration through defamiliarisation. Even though the audience was

86 *Dating directing*

Figure 4.2 Georgia Metternick-Jones (2013), set (from *No Worries*)
Photographer: Soseh Yekanians

Figure 4.3 Hannah Metternick-Jones (2013), costume sketches (from *No Worries*)

familiar with these objects, by re-using them in a heightened state on the stage, I was able to bring new meaning to them once contextualised within the whole play.

In *Uncle Jack*, I took a similar stance when it came to the costumes and set. Again, none of these directorial choices of set or clothing was initiated by Lonnie. Once more, I littered the stage with dirt to represent outback Australia and utilised the same handmade wooden boxes as depicted in Figure 4.2 from *No Worries* to give an authentic rural feel to the furniture. Scattered around the space were longnecks, billycans and props iconic to the Australian outback. The character of Uncle Jack, similar to the narrator in *No Worries*, wore the clichéd KingGee shorts, singlet and boots (see Figure 4.4), and the character Doug remained in a version of a recognisable Australian army officers' uniform throughout the play (see Figure 4.5).

Additionally, in both plays, I encouraged the actors not to neutralise their Australian accents but instead to heighten them to amplify the flat Australian sound. This also facilitated the idea of stereotypical Australia even further. These requests seemed comical and over the top to the actors at the time; however, they represented the Australia that I had constructed to help me simplify and categorise the world (Australia) and the play (Hinton, 2000). I realised that, to bring weight to the key moments, I needed to take the "objects", as Shklovsky (1917) would say, and use the technique of defamiliarisation to bring significance to the audience's everyday recognition of the common articles, which may have lost their importance in the present day. This approach highlighted the play's issues in an effort to encourage the audiences to see the objects in a new light (Shklovsky, 1917).

However, it is vital to remember that to make defamiliarisation work, the objects (characters, props, set, scenery, language) need to be imbued with integrity and honesty to prevent them from becoming mere caricatures or parodies of their recognisable ideas. For example, in *No Worries*, had I exaggerated the narrator's role to the point where it became comical, it would have prevented the audience from listening and absorbing his narration. His role was vital in *No Worries*, as it created an intimate

Figure 4.4 Production still (2014) (from *Uncle Jack*)
Photographer: Soseh Yekanians

88 *Dating directing*

Figure 4.5 Production still (2014) (from *Uncle Jack*)
Photographer: Soseh Yekanians

relationship with the audience, introducing the main characters of the story, and propelled us into Matilda's journey. I understood that with both plays, if I had endlessly mocked or pushed the boundaries of reality too far, the defamiliarisation process would have not worked and instead, the audience would have felt ridiculed and the *message* within the pieces would have been lost and may have instead offended.

Contiguous to creating audience familiarity with the themes in a play arises the quandary of how to keep audiences not only emotionally engaged with the action of the scene(s) on stage but also empathetic towards the characters. This is a major obstacle and objective in itself; for directors to assume that an emotion can be simply imposed upon the audience is both naïve and unrealistic. Therefore, in the same way that defamiliarisation helps audiences see a familiar object in a new light, I wondered if this objective could influence audiences in an emotional capacity. David Miall and Don Kuiken (1994), developing Shklovsky's (1917) ideas of defamiliarisation, believed that it can. They understood that the effect of defamiliarisation can be transferred onto an audience's emotions when correctly employed. Miall and Kuiken (1994) explored the use of defamiliarisation in relation to feelings and emotions through Samuel Taylor Coleridge's ideas of defamiliarisation in his literary works. Coleridge (1817) first used the term defamiliarisation in *Biographia Literaria* in reference to his ideas of poetic imagination and observation. He claimed that defamiliarisation "dissolves, diffuses, dissipates, in order to re-create the familiar" (p. 304). Coleridge maintained that defamiliarisation is concerned with "exciting the sympathy of the reader by a faithful adherence to the truth of nature" (p. 5). He went on to say that the power of the technique is that it gives the audience the interest of novelty by modifying the colours of their imagination once again. Therefore, while defamiliarisation assists in making familiar objects "new" again, at the same time, the technique stimulates people's imaginations and evokes new emotions within their previous and current understandings.

To explore this concept, I searched for moments within my private life when I had had emotional experiences similar to those of the characters. An illustration of this is in Act Two of *No Worries*. In one of the scenes, the city students are bullying Matilda Bell and her friend Binh for their racial differences (Matilda being Indigenous Australian and Binh a Vietnamese refugee). Even though Holman had often been quoted as saying that *No Worries* was for big kids of all ages, initially, as a TIE play, it had been specifically written for young primary school audiences. Therefore, the scenes were composed in a lighter way rather than how I was directing them, which was aimed at a much older adult audience. I wanted the play, but particularly this scene, to have a strong effect on the audience and evoke feelings in them of a threat from the bullies and desolation for Matilda and Binh. To highlight the significance of this moment within the play, I used my personal experiences of being bullied to bring gravitas and importance to that specific scene and to the underlying theme. In rehearsals with the cast, I communicated how I was bullied because of my ethnic appearance and how it had affected me growing up. I then asked the cast to empathise and share their direct or witnessed experiences of cultural discrimination, either towards themselves or in situations they had witnessed. Once we had conversed extensively on this subject, I attempted to direct the physical representation of the scene in a way that not only almost paralleled my first-hand experience of being harassed at school but also resembled the intimate occurrences the cast had discussed. For instance, one of the actors physically demonstrated how she was bullied at school because of her mixed racial appearance; the other kids often did not play or sit with her at lunch. In fact, they would walk past her whispering and then waving their hands asking, "Can you understand English, mate?" That feeling of exclusion and ridicule she described was the decisive inspiration behind how I blocked the scene in which Matilda is introduced to her new city school for the first time, and the "city kids" laugh at her indigenous appearance (see Figure 4.6).

Unlike *No Worries*, in which I had been able to find some familiarisation with the play's themes, *Uncle Jack* presented me with difficulties in finding commonalities or even resonance with either of the characters in the story, alongside its central themes of Anzac Day and PTSD. Instead, I managed to find an association with the emotions that arise in the aftermath of the ravages of war. The varied emotions this story stimulated in me were not new but indeed went back to my youth. As an adolescent who was learning Armenian and Australian history simultaneously, I recall asking my father several times on Anzac Day, "What about us – when will

90 *Dating directing*

Figure 4.6 Production still (2013) (from *No Worries*)
Photographer: Soseh Yekanians

anyone remember what happened to us?" I knew that to find inspiration as a director I would need to revisit and review the undesirable emotions I had towards this day. I recognised that no matter how deep my adversities ran, I needed to remain fair-minded and professional and do Lonnie's story justice.

According to Bourdieu (1977, 1984), focusing on one's cultural identity and concentrating on differences (or distinctions), at times, blinds one to the possibility of the similarities. Bourdieu (1984) suggested that the development of one's sense of the game, through engagement with particular ideas and identities, may cloud one's ability to see the unexpected. His thoughts echo those of Shklovsky (1917, 1990), who suggested it was through our differences that we at times find the similarities that help us to convey and connect with a particular story. In turn, this allows audiences to understand and perceive key moments or themes in a new light. Closer to Bourdieu's (1984) views on difference, however, are those of French theorist Jacques Derrida (1968, 1982). Although Derrida's arguments on difference directly concern text and semantic reduction, as is the case with Shklovsky's (1917) ideas, the leap across to directing is not that steep because the disciplines carry comparable dramatic attributes of storytelling.

Derrida's (1982) approach to difference examines how the perceiver's mental state is constantly in a state of flux and therefore differs from one reading of a text to the next or from one general theory to another, making the *real* understanding of the work unachievable (as cited in Norris, 2002). Derrida

(1982) understood that, instead, difference is temporal and so is our relationship towards a text. He asserted, "Since the trace is not a presence but a *simulacrum of a presence, that dislocates itself, refers itself, it properly has no site – erasure belongs to its structure*" (p. 22, italics in original). Therefore, to read any material or have one absolute understanding of one moment is impossible because difference, as Derrida (1982) understood it, requires us to open ourselves up to the idea that a range of possibilities and understandings may be connected to that reading or, rather, a given moment in a play. This notion was summed up beautifully by Roland Pada (2007) when he wrote that difference is the activity of "offending its *past*, and at the same time its *future* in order to make *present* come into the fore of our thoughts in the fleeting singularity of time" (p. 48, italics in original). Identification of difference in *Uncle Jack* caused my temporality towards the story to change dramatically. And so, although none of the members of my family had fought in Gallipoli or suffered the traumas of PTSD, by overlooking my initial bias and assumptions and instead, on route with Bourdieu's (1984) and Derrida's (1982) advice, refocusing my emotions towards the camaraderie shared between the Armenians and the Australians who were combating an analogous losing battle, the similarities arose. By the end of the first week of rehearsals, I had developed a real tenderness and appreciation for Lonnie's narrative and its characters. What made *Uncle Jack* a successful experience was that, for the first time, I genuinely recognised how my difference as an individual assisted in my direction of a piece. Although I may not have found a strong association with the particular iconic Australian representation of the Anzac story or the characters, I was able to produce an emotional response to the premise of the story by transference and juxtaposition of my personal emotions towards my cultural heritage. This gave me, as the director, a way into the crux of the play and assisted in creating the emotional weight on the stage that the narrative of war deserved.

During his interview, Neeme spoke of the director's identity often being mixed with the personal emotions one carries. He said,

> *Inevitably the choices we tend to make and our view of the world will colour our work, so we don't need to strive in this direction. On the contrary, we need to guard against these instinctive/unthinking responses, and place them under more stringent scrutiny. Thus attempting to ensure that we reaching out to the work in hand and not just reducing it to what we already know.*
>
> (Interview, 20 August 2013)

Similarly, Tan advised,

> *I think it takes a bit of detachment and the ability to see yourself from the outside in order to learn about yourself and your identity. We are full of bias about our own selves and sometimes the creative process may even cause an "unbalanced" person to struggle with their own identity even more. It's a fine*

> line. If however you have an open and curious attitude, then yes I think you can discover and affirm your identity through your work.
>
> (Interview, 6 August 2013)

Revisiting these interviews and hearing the directors' thoughts regarding detachment as a director or guarding against one's instinctive emotional response towards a story proved timely. My emotional engagement with *No Worries* and *Uncle Jack* were accessed differently, yet that did not change my role as the director within the group or the "journey" I had as the director. The almost cathartic experience of going through the director's journey with a cast mentioned by many of the directors I interviewed was still achieved through this process of difference. In fact, as articulated by Tan (Interview, 6 August 2013), via the detachment and differences, as a director, I gained the ability to see myself from a new perspective, and in doing so, I learnt about aspects of myself and my identity through this new approach.

I think the methods of defamiliarisation, even though initially used by Shklovsky (1917) as poetic devices for language and difference, as understood by Bourdieu (1977, 1984) and Derrida (1982) in relation to text, can be employed by directors in their rehearsal rooms as powerful visual and emotional tools to help them achieve their director's vision. I have no doubt that defamiliarisation and fluidity of difference allowed me to highlight the play's foremost issues of racism (*No Worries*) and the emotional ramifications of war (*Uncle Jack*) so that Australian audiences who were already familiar with the stories' themes, and possibly wearied by them, could see these themes and objects in a new light – their senses emotionally engaged via this new perspective. Moreover, I learnt to appreciate that as directors and as artists, we do not need to come from a specific world in order to create or recreate that world. In fact, in both instances, my migrant Australian status without familiarisation and my learnt stereotypical relationship and understanding of Australia enabled me to *make strange* the familiar. In doing so, I was able to highlight the distinctions in the plays that a director directly or culturally acquainted with the stories may not have perceived rather than underplay the key representations of the plays' central themes, as the actors had wanted.

Notes

1 "Through-line" is a Practical Aesthetics term, which means "the single overriding action that all the individual actions serve" (Nadel, 2008, p. 44). The through-line unites the overall objective of the entire story. Within the play, there are scenes that have multiple objectives. The playwright, actor or character and director all have clear mini-objectives, which in turn continually work (scene by scene) to achieve the overall through-line of the story.
2 "Creatives" is the unofficial theatrical term given to the team of creative individuals and other staff members who assist directors in reaching their creative objectives. The core of this team usually consists of the stage managers (and their assistants), the production managers, the costume and set designers, the lighting and sound designers and the other contributing members of the production team.

3 The term "defamiliarisation" was introduced by Viktor Shklovsky in his 1917 essay *Art as Technique* and is at times referred to in its Russian form as *ostranenie*.
4 This is a long-necked bottle of beer, also known as a "longneck stubby", and it is iconic to the Australian culture (TripAdvisor, 2015).

References

Allport, G. W. (1954). *The nature of prejudice*. Boston, MA: Addison-Wesley Publishing Company.
Artaud, A. (1958). *The theater and its double*. New York: Grove Press, Inc.
Benedetti, L. R. (1985). *The director at work*. Upper Saddle River, NJ: Prentice-Hall, Inc.
Blount-Nuss, G. (2011). *The effects of stereotype threat on state levels of stigma consciousness and overall performance on stereotype-relevant task*. Master of Science, Georgia Southern University, United States. Retrieved from http://digitalcommons.georgiasouthern.edu/cgi/viewcontent.cgi?article=1440&context=etd
Bogart, A. (2001). *A director prepares: Seven essays on art and theatre*. London: Routledge.
Bourdieu, P. (1977). *An outline of a theory of practice*. Cambridge: Cambridge University Press.
Bourdieu, P. (1984). *Distinction: A social critique of the judgement of taste*. Cambridge, MA: Harvard University Press.
Brecht, B. (1977). *Brecht on theatre: The development of an aesthetic*. New York: Hill and Wang.
Brockett, O. G., & Hildy, F. J. (1999). *History of the theatre* (8th ed.). Boston, MA: Allyn & Bacon.
Bruch, D. (1990). Directing theatre. *Debra Bruch*. Retrieved from http://dbruch.hypermart.net/engineer/direct.html
Bruder, M., Cohn, L. M., Olnek, M., Pollack, N., Previto, R. & Zigler, S. (1986). *A practical handbook for the actor*. New York, NY: Random House.
Cohen, R. (2011). *Working together in theatre: Collaboration and leadership*. New York: Palgrave Macmillan.
Cole, S. L. (1992). *Directors in rehearsal: A hidden world*. New York: Routledge.
Cole, T., & Chinoy, H.-K. (1953). *Directors on directing: A source book of the modern theatre* London: Peter Owen Limited.
Coleridge, S. T. (1817). *Biographia literaria* (J. Engell & W. J. Bate, Eds.). London: Routledge.
Corliss, R. (1985, July 15). "I dream for a living": Steven Spielberg, the prince of Hollywood, is still a little boy at heart. *Time Magazine*, pp. 1–7.
Cropp, M. (2005). Lost tragedies: A survey. In J. Gregory (Ed.), *A companion to Greek tragedy*. Malden, MA: Wiley-Blackwell.
Derrida, J. (1968). Difference. In *Margins of philosophy*. Paris: Editions du Seuil.
Derrida, J. (1982). *Margins of philosophy*. Chicago, IL: University of Chicago Press.
Dobson, G., Murray, D., Lindsay, M., Teh, T.-Y., Broun, A., & Mooney, P. (2013). *Lifted*! [Theatre]. Perth: The Kitchen Sink Collective.
Erikson, E. H. (1963a). *Childhood and society*. New York: W. W. Norton & Company Inc.
Erikson, E. H. (1963b). *Youth change and challenge*. New York: Basic Books.
Friedman, S. S. (2004). Bodies on the move: A poetics of home and diaspora. *Tulsa Studies in Women's Literature*, *23*(2), 189–212.
Gregory, W. A. (1968). *The director: A guide to modern theater practice*. New York: Funk & Wagnalls, A Division of Reader's Digest Books, Inc.
Hinton, P. D. (2000). *Stereotypes, cognition and culture*. New York: Psychology Press.
Holman, D. (1989). *No worries*. Sydney, Australia: Currency Press.

Lippmann, W. (1922). *Public opinion*. New York: Harcourt Press.
Lonnie, R. (2014). *Uncle Jack*. Perth, Australia: Ross Lonnie.
Mamet, D. (2010). *Theatre*. New York: Faber Inc.
Miall, D. S., & Kuiken, D. (1994). Foregrounding, defamiliarization, and affect: Response to literary stories. *Poetics, 22*, 389–407.
Mitchell, K. (2008). *The director's craft: A handbook for the theatre*. New York: Routledge.
Nadel, I. (2008). *David Mamet: A life in the theatre*. New York, NY: Palgrave Macmillan.
Norris, C. (2002). *Deconstruction: Theory and practice* (3rd ed.). London: Routledge.
Pada, R. T. S. (2007). The paradox of ipseity and difference: Derrida's deconstruction and logocentrism. *KRITIKĒ, 1*(1), 32–51.
Pearsall, J., & Hanks, P. (Eds.). (2010). *Oxford dictionary of English* (3rd ed.). Oxford: Oxford University Press.
Pike, S. (2014). *Yesterday's hero* [Theatre]. Perth: The Kitchen Sink Collective.
Roose-Evans, J. (1970). *Experimental theatre: From Stanislavsky to Peter Brook* (4th ed.). London: Routledge.
Schultz, D. P., & Schultz, S. E. (2008). *Theories of personality* (9th ed.). Belmont, CA: Wadsworth Cengage Learning.
Shklovsky, V. (1917). Art as technique. In D. H. Richter (Ed.), *The critical tradition: Classic texts and contemporary trends* (3rd ed., pp. 774–785). Boston, MA and New York: Bedford/St. Martin's.
Shklovsky, V. (1990). *Theory of prose*. Champaign and London: Dalkey Archive Press.
Stanislavski, C. (1962). *Stanislavsky my life in art* (J. J. Robbins, Trans.). New York: Geoffrey Bles, Ltd.
TripAdvisor. (2015). *Australia: Culture*. Retrieved 3 March 2015 from http://www.tripadvisor.com.au/TravelJg255055Js202/Australia:Culture.html
Trumbull, D. E. W. (2008). Introduction to theatre: The Director. *NOVA, Northern Virginia Community College*. Retrieved from www.novaonline.nvcc.edu/eli/spd130et/director.htm
Various (Writer). (1985–present). *Neighbours* [Television]. J. Herdison & L. Wilson (Producers). Australia: Grundy Television.
Various (Writer). (1988–present). *Home and Away* [Television]. J. Holmes & L. Addario (Producers). Australia: Red Heart Entertainment.
Ward, P. (1988, November 26–27). The whiz of Les Miserables: An interview with Australian theatre director Gale Edwards. *The Australian*, pp. 11–12.

Conclusion

When considering the variety of factors that influenced this doctoral research, it was simple for me to forget that, in the beginning, I was purely a theatre director who wanted to deepen her understanding of the creative art form of directing. This platform presented as an ideal vehicle for gaining subjective insights into my role as a theatre director and the field of directing. There were substantial scholarly texts surrounding directing and how the director's role came to have its contemporary standing. These scholarly texts, however, did not satisfy my deeper curiosities regarding my love of directing and the stimuli behind its pursuit. I had forgotten that my journey into the profession had begun with a strong attraction to the theatre.

Chapter 1, "Attracted to Theatre: Setting the Scene", revealed the possibilities behind this attraction. In the distant past, theatre was used as a method of storytelling and a way to express ritualistic ways of daily life. Through the representations on stage of stories and myths, audiences are affected and will reflect upon their own lives. The theatre as a social experience can be easily conceived as a powerful vessel for storytelling and exploration.

Was that what had attracted me? It was then that the research widened into an exploration and rediscovery of my own provocations for pursuing this creative path. In doing so, I needed to explore all facets of my identity.

To undertake this exploration, a thorough literature review of scholarly and philosophic notions surrounding identity in a contemporary context was required. Hence, as presented in Chapter 2, "Seeking Identity: Searching for Self", I set out to discover through various theorists and psychologists what identity is and how it is constructed. Through this avenue of research, considerable material came to light and informed the study. Some experts regard identity as not static but, instead, always in a state of development and contingent on the individual's environment at the time. Conversely, identity formation also instigates loss of identity or *identity crisis*. During the period of adolescence when an individual begins to experiment with different roles and ideologies to try to determine the most compatible fit, failure to complete this process results in a form of *identity crisis*. At this stage, individuals take a lengthy look into how they are viewed within the world and fittingly look for new opportunities of expression. These insights were vital for the research to come.

Words such as *displacement*, *other*, *belonging*, *unhomely* and *in-between* all began to shift my naïve outlook to a more informed perspective. The significance of these notions led me to additional academic scholars who discussed at length these key ideas.

Commonly, but not always, these notions are recognised through cultural difference and diaspora. Yet while these concepts overwhelmingly initiate loss of identity, they are also positive attributes that help to reconstruct a person's new sense of identity. With a willingness to inspect these attributes in direct connection to my motivations, I knew that the first step would be to scrutinise my ethnic identity as an Armenian.

Chapter 3, "Affinity with Armenia: A Narrative in Two Parts", endeavoured to contextualise the history of Armenia but also provide insights into my heritage. This period of exploration was not easy, nor was it comfortable, as it forced me to look at my strained allegiance towards my culture. More significantly, it forced me to re-examine the pain that I had often felt when confronted with the atrocities of the ancient land, such as the 1915 Armenian Genocide and its present-day denial. Considerations then turned towards my 2008 trip to Armenia and then my return trip in 2014. In 2008, not experiencing the wonderful results that I had hoped for, as occurred with so many other Armenians, left me feeling dejected, ashamed and rejected for not being a *real* Armenian. The persistent animosity that had begun on the first trip was now clouding my judgement as a researcher. This is why, in 2014, as part of the academic journey, I travelled back. With my newfound empathies, on this occasion, the voyage stimulated a renewed appreciation in me as an Armenian. Upon returning, I knew that I needed to explore these transformations further as a theatre director and storyteller.

A more informed perspective initiated the formation of purposeful methodological foundations for the main areas of investigation. By developing methods specifically tailored towards directing practice, such as the interviews with the directors and the immersion into my practice as a director, my aim was to gain a deeper perceptive into the nuances behind the field of theatre directing and investigate the potential links. Through open-ended interviews, I was able to elicit from these generous research participants principal findings on their discernments surrounding the director role. These interviews were pivotal in the discovery of new insights into and comprehensions of theatre directing, and they provided fresh considerations that assisted in formulating the rest of the study.

A two-part construction of the interviews allowed the research to advance into questioning how theatre directing can provide a person with a sense of identity and belonging and in some way address the internal struggles often encountered because of cultural displacement.

Phase 1 began to show promising results and revealed probable motivations behind choosing the profession of theatre directing. The interviews began to uncover key characteristics of the participants that would lead them to become *directors*. A number of participants interviewed suggested that a great director has qualities of leadership that inspire and unite the actors towards a common goal. The individual needs to possess a great degree of confidence, vision and imagination, as well as the ability to engage in genuine responses with the cast. Several interviewees indicated their strong belief that a director should come up through the ranks and earn the right to call her/himself a director. Some, however, remained wary of people who claimed they were directors without directing credentials or a creative curriculum vitae. Further inquiries into the background of the director revealed that directing, unlike other careers in the creative industries, commonly does not require prerequisites or proof of qualifications per se. The directors interviewed did not receive formal training but, in its place, learnt and developed their craft by observing other directors with whom they worked. Many of these directors had deliberately not considered formal training, as they wanted to develop their own style. Additionally, some directors suggested that directors rarely choose to be directors in the first place and so never actually seek training. Rather, the interviewed directors

1 transitioned into the role of the director through acting,
2 fell naturally into directing through coincidence or suggestions made by the other actors with whom they were working at the time, or
3 were unexpectedly thrust into directing without time to *learn* or consider the position.

The transitioning factor in particular was fascinating, as it resounded with my personal experiences. Further questioning into how the transition into theatre directing occurred, but more significantly why it happened, revealed three key motivators that stimulated the directors' shift:

1 Directing gave them a sense of community and purpose.
2 Directing gave them better control of their artistic expression.
3 Directing gave them a platform for their voices and opinions and provided agency.

For the most part, the directing profession was non-judgemental of cultural differences. Cultural differences in the theatre seemed to be celebrated.

A breakdown of these answers began to address how theatre directing can provide a sense of belonging and a (re)discovered sense of identity.

Community and belonging are words that arose at various points in the interviews. Most directors noted that for people who have struggled with any form of displacement in their lives, directing provides them with a sense of belonging and engagement. Community is generally engaged with in two ways: in the rehearsal room working with the actors and creatives and in the performance via the audiences that the director's work has reached. The majority of directors felt that as the process of directing is not solitary, the sense of belonging and community is created through the strong appreciation of working with others and having a clear position within a team. Within the rehearsal room, the directors have a certain level of responsibility, and everyone is observing them as chief leader. This level of responsibility gives the directors drive and authority within their role but

98 Conclusion

equally creates a sense of being, place and purpose. During the interviews, many directors communicated that if that sense of *being* is absent from their personal lives, as directors, the sentiments are enough to make them feel as if they belong to *something*. This sense of purpose was articulated repetitively by the directors and became a pivotal finding in Phase 1.

Directors asserted that beyond directing being a collaborative vocation that is dependent on other individuals on the team, the depth of those relationships holds the most significance. Many directors related that rarely in their experience had another profession offered them the intimacy and openness that directing does. This is in part due to the intimate stories that are often shared between the cast and creatives, contributing to the director's own need for artistic expression. Artistic expression and a platform to explore individuality are key phrases that almost all directors reiterated. All the directors interviewed had transitioned in one way or another from acting. Directing had provided these directors with a fresh challenge and more opportunities for artistic control over their work, but it had also given them agency as individuals. Suddenly as directors, matters concerning cultural differences and stereotypes that they were accustomed to as actors had lessened. Instead, directing had provided a platform for individual expression and a sense of agency. These facets of agency and expression were fascinating and underscored by the sense of community and family that in turn developed.

From Phase 1, answers to questions into the director's journey had begun to surface. Further questions in Phase 2 set out to uncover the fundamentals or mechanics behind the director's journey. The breakdown of the interviews suggested that the process of directing is an infinite spiral of endless creativity. After directors begin a new play with a new group of people, inevitably, they leave that group and then begin the process again with a new play and a new set of actors. Interestingly, most directors appreciated this facet of the process and did not have difficulty moving on to the next play. While they often felt like they were on a repetitive journey, they valued that the lessons and experiences learnt in production are inevitably carried into each new work. The nomadic aspect of the journey resembles that of a wanderer. The director, like the individual, continually searches for belonging and perfection in a fixed location (the play) only to realise that often what they seek is an elusive imaginary setting. It appears that directors only ever attain a small degree of freedom in mind, as they can never feel anything other than that they are wanderers within the structure of the theatre. However, because of the nomadic nature of the profession, they are required not to fixate on one cast or one story but instead to let go of previous ideas, making fresh sense of each new work. I began to ask further questions of the research:

1   If directing is in itself an unhoming profession, then how is belonging and identity achieved?
2   Is it through the activity and process of directing or the plays that the director selected?

Before commencing my research, I anticipated that I would discover that directors find a sense of identity through the stories they tell. It is via these stories that directors are then able to recreate an imaginary world unique to them, steeped in their individuality and creative expression. When the directors were interviewed on this matter, the answers revealed that the sense of self is reflected not in the plays but in the activity of directing. The finality of the *play* is a by-product of the creative process and a necessary outcome of the director's work. Several directors related anecdotes of cautioning other directors who purposely set out to *find themselves* through the plays they were directing. Many directors articulated that directors need to guard strongly against the instinctive or unthinking responses that the play may raise. Instead, they should reposition those emotions and examine them more stringently, thus attempting to ensure that as directors, they are reaching out to the work at hand and not just reducing the story to what they already know. Commonly, it is through these differences or distinctions that the director then begins to develop and grow.

Relatedly, though in opposition, several directors, while confirming the importance of detachment, stated that throughout their careers, they had frequently found themselves directing plays that dealt with familiar themes that mirrored their personal lives. They reiterated that the plays to which they are drawn usually reflect personal experiences and help them to understand their own lives and themselves better. As I had only experienced directing plays whose story lines I had connections with, these deliberations were thought provoking.

No Worries and *Uncle Jack* presented perfect opportunities for me as a director. I was in a position to direct two plays whose overarching narratives and representations of stereotypical Australia I connected with but in a tangential way. These plays gave me a chance to explore, via my own immersion into directing, how the differences that the directors had spoken of assist me in finding new appreciations within the role and to allow the academic literature to inform new rehearsal methods. The process of directing these plays was perplexing at first. This was partly due to my own bias from my preconceived ideas about what plays directors should (and can) direct. However, it was also through this collaborative process that I recognised that my subjective experiences of being *othered* might not in fact have been that special. Instead, the theatre allowed me to notice that the themes that I believed were unique to me were in fact themes that many individuals experienced. Equally, my previous assumptions that directing plays close to one's own story carries more significance were also discredited. No matter the narrative, the activity of directing and the journey with the team remains the same; the only differences are the methods I employ in achieving the results and that the discoveries are enhanced and expanded. In fact, adapting the literary devices of *defamiliarisation* and *difference* as new methods of exploration not only provided me with career-altering experiences but also led me to produce two successful productions that challenged my former beliefs. This leads to the overall conclusion that it is the activity of directing that generates the sense of community, purpose, belonging and individualistic voice and not exclusively the stories or play.

By the end of the two-phase interview process, it was evident from the directors interviewed that theatre directing provides an individual with a sense of belonging through the sentiments of community and purpose that it generates. (Re)discovery of the individual's identity is realised through the empowering and authoritative nature of the profession. By placing individuals in the role of leader and giving them agency, directing provides them with a platform to express their distinctive ideas in a forum that is, for the most part, non-judgemental.

Although I may not have answered all the questions surrounding the director's role, I do think the interviews conducted with the respected theatre directors offered unprecedented insight into the possible incentives that the director's role can give individuals who have struggled with their sense of purpose and self. With this in mind, extending the research would entail a more complicated construction of questions and perhaps a broader range of industry professionals, such as film directors. It would be fascinating to probe deeper into the psyches of those who follow a profession into all areas of directing and the performing arts to uncover whether the primal need of belonging and community is what draws them in. Do directing and the arts at all levels offer a sense of family and expression of individual voice or is this limited to theatre directing? Extending the research with more data to create a thorough understanding of all areas in the creative arts might lead to more national recognition of their importance and thus increase future arts funding and repute.

Looking into new areas of extension, as a theatre director-researcher, I am captivated by the idea of cultural stereotyping and its transparency (or lack thereof) within the Australian environment. Each culture, whether intentionally or otherwise, has various signifiers already associated with that culture – that is, the codes, rituals and language systems. I would argue that there are certain inherent inequities and forms of discrimination that, no matter how hard we try to rise above them, whether through education, environment, economics or domestic location, we cannot escape. I hope that my continued work as a researcher will convey alternatives that will provide insights into and assistance towards intercultural understandings.

Final thoughts

Recalling my 7-year-old self in my father's Armenian play *The Dog and the Cat*, I appear to have always been attracted to the theatre while simultaneously trying to find some lucidity of who I am as an individual. Although this research began with my subjective queries about why I was attracted to directing and how I believed it helped me, eventually, by asking these questions of others, I began to gain innate appreciations of the role of the theatre director. Looking back on this academic journey, I can appreciate why that immovable place of dwelling, of which I was in constant pursuit for so long, and that singular way of being do not in fact exist. For although I may feel more Armenian in Armenia (as much as my Persian-Armenian status will allow) or more Armenian around my traditions or when I am speaking the language, it does not devalue my sense of being an Australian.

My identity is constructed of the complexities and chaos of my entire tri-cultural heritage, and that disorder embodies my unique expression and work as a theatre director. Just as a director's work is a boundless spiral of self-critic creation, so is my pursuit of persona within myself and the society in which I live. However, the theatre, as a transformative space that celebrates differences, and directing, as a commanding yet communal profession that allows individual expression, seem like the perfect spaces to keep examining these complex matters. Maybe in our willingness to re-examine our abilities more deeply as theatre directors, we have the opportunity to understand ourselves better as human beings and, through the activity of theatre directing, begin to share these experiences with others.

Appendix

Interview questions from phase 1

1. Where were you born?
2. (If not Australia) How old were you when you came to Australia?
3. Where did you grow up?
4. Have you always wanted to be a theatre director?
5. If not, what was your profession beforehand?
6. How did you get into theatre directing?
7. What do you think attracted you to theatre directing?
8. How and where did you learn or train to be a theatre director?
9. What methods of directing do you use in your rehearsal room?
10. How did you come to develop or form these methods?
11. As a director, I think that the environment of a rehearsal room is a direct result of its director. What are your thoughts on this?
12. How is your interaction with people in your daily life different or similar to your manner as a theatre director?
13. Do you feel then that your identity as a director differentiates between your identity as an individual?
14. What do you think makes a good director?
15. What do you think makes a great director?
16. If I asked if are you a playwright-driven director, an audience-driven director or an ego-driven director, what would you say?
17. If you were born or even raised outside of Australia, have you ever struggled with a sense of identity or belonging within Australia?
18. Would you be happy or fulfilled doing any other profession?
19. What are the core elements that theatre directing gives an individual that they may not receive in any other profession?
20. Renowned Australian theatre director Gayle Edwards said, "Being a director can be a very hard job: it's lonely, it's isolated, you are responsible if anything goes wrong, you are forgotten when everything goes right, you're attacked by critics". How do you feel about that? Do you agree or disagree? If you agree, then why do you think you kept pursuing the path of directing?

21 Do you feel that you're attracted to certain types of plays/works? If so, what attracts you to a play? Is this a conscious decision?
22 Do you believe that as directors we are possibly drawn to certain types of plays because they give us a chance to investigate our own personal identities through the work?
23 Do you knowingly strive to put "yourself" into a piece you direct, or do you feel this naturally happens? What are your thoughts on this?
24 Do you feel that there may be a common thread or commonality between your cultural drive and investigations in who you are as an individual and your personal motivations for becoming a theatre director?
25 Does directing give you a sense of belonging? If so, has this helped you find a deeper sense of belonging within the wider world in which you are situated?
26 Do you think individuals who have struggled with their own sense of identity and belonging can somehow find their answers or clarifications in their *selves* through the creative pursuit of theatre directing? If so, how and why do you think this elucidation occurs?
27 What I love about my work as a director is that it's not only my unique vision that I am able to project onto a story, but, for the most part, I know people will look at the final play and see "Soseh the director's show". Not "Soseh the Armenian-Persian-Australian". Do you find a similar connection to that at all? If so, do you think, possibly, that may be where the attraction or addiction to theatre directing may lie?
28 Is there anything else you would like to add to the thoughts, concerns or comments I have asked or discussed during the interview?

Interview questions from phase 2

1 What do you think are three unique qualities that theatre directing provides individuals that they may not find in another vocation?
2 When a director embarks on a new play, do you think s/he begins some form of a journey?
3 What are the most significant points along this journey that you have experienced as a theatre director?
4 For many directors, directing provides them with a sense of belonging. What do you think is the main instigator of this?
5 Do you feel it is the personal journey that a director goes through that provides her/him with a sense identity? Or do you think it comes via the action of directing or both?
6 Do you think an individual who has felt displacement can find a better sense of her/his identity or a sense of belonging through directing?
7 What would you say is the main reason for this?
8 Has directing helped you find either identity or a sense of belonging?
9 Has directing helped you find your place within the wider community and maybe in turn your place in the world? Have you ever thought about this?
10 Is directing, or in fact performing arts in general, an addictive line of work?

11 What do you think is the main cause of the addiction?
12 Some actors have a hard time letting go of productions they've been a part of, as a director, do you have a hard time letting go?
13 When do you think your role as a director ends?
14 Not all, but most, directors transition into directing from acting; in fact, it is often said, "You don't choose directing, it chooses you". What do you think about this statement?
15 What are the three most attractive qualities that directing provides a creative individual that s/he may not receive through acting?
16 Why do you think directing is still such an elusive art form within the performing arts?
17 Do you think the role of the director is a necessary one, and if so, why?
18 Do you believe anyone can be a director? Please discuss.
19 Is there anything else you would like to add to the thoughts, concerns or comments I have asked or discussed during the interview?

Full list of theatre directors interviewed

Phase 1

Chuck Hudson	*Interviewed 11 October 2012*
Pearl Tan	*Interviewed 6 August 2013*
Lex Marinos OAM	*Interviewed 16 August 2013*
Aarne Neeme AM	*Interviewed 20 August 2013*
Ira Seidenstein	*Interviewed 20 August 2013*
Joseph Uchitel	*Interviewed 2 September 2013*
Bianca Bagatourian	*Interviewed 11 September 2013*
Frederick Copperwaite	*Interviewed 11 September 2013*
Jean-Pierre Mignon	*Interviewed 14 September 2013*
John Kachoyan	*Interviewed 28 October 2013*
Netta Yashchin	*Interviewed 10 December 2013*
James Denalli	*Interviewed 3 April 2014*

Phase 2

Anthony Skuse	*Interviewed 16 February 2014*
Gabrielle Metcalf	*Interviewed 6 March 2014*
Denise Eden	*Interviewed 14 March 2014*
Sam Cleary	*Interviewed 15 March 2014*
Barney Gibbs	*Interviewed 18 March 2014*
Steven Truscott	*Interviewed 18 March 2014*
Nicole Cervonaro	*Interviewed 23 March 2014*
Anthony Yarra	*Interviewed 27 March 2014*
Stephanie Glover	*Interviewed 2 April 2014*
Tan Ataya	*Interviewed 9 April 2014*

Index

Note: Page numbers in *italics* denote figures on the corresponding page.

տուն 31
ճակատագիր 19, 26–27

Achebe, Chinua 85
acting 20, 68–72; to directing, transitioning from 81, 97–98, 104; exercises 30; and identity 24; school 66–67
acting teacher-director 39
actor 17, 29–30; and character 29; multicultural 73; and non-actor 19; psyche of 18–19; selfhood of 20; training 67; *see also* Binoche, Juliette; Cher
actor-director 39
Adalian, Rouben Paul 44
Aeschylus 64
Alamuddin Clooney, Amal 50
Allport, Gordon 85
Alony, Irit 8
Anzacs 82, 91
Anzac Day 89
Archer, William 30
apology 59
Arab 45–46, 60
Armenia: birth of 44–46; culture and cultural heritage of 19, 21, 26; home, concept of 31; as homeland 31, 54; independence 51–52; invasion of 46–47; under Iranian rule 13; New Armenia 44, 55–61; post-Soviet 51; returning to Australia from 54–55; traveling from Australia to 51–54, 60; *see also* ճակատագիր; Karabakh
Armenian-Australian identity 3, 5, 35, 38, 51; *see also* Persian-Armenian-Australian, identity
Armenian communities 2–3, 21
Armenian diaspora *see* diaspora (Armenian)

Armenian Genocide 3, 45, 47–51, 61, 82, 96
Armenian identity *see* identity
Artaud, Antonin 14, 16, 19–20, 73
Artsakh *see* Karabakh
assimilation 28, 35, 45, 60
Assyria 44, 46
Ataya, Tan 104
Atlantic Theater Company Acting School 13
Australia 2, 49; actors in 73; culture of 38, 100; directors from/in 10–11, 70–71; and genocide 49–50; as home 31; immigrating to 13; outback 82, 86–87
"Aussie" 21, 38–39, 84
Australian/Australians (people) 1; accents 87; appearance of 74; humour of 39–40; identity 100; indigenous 89; migrant 92; as nationality 35–37, 52; stereotypical 21, 82–92, 99
"Australiana" 85
Australian Academy of Dramatic Art 13
autoethnography 2, 6, 8–9
Azerbaijan 51, 56–58

Bagatourian, Bianca 67, 70, 74, 104
Bagratid Dynasty 46
Beck, Aaron Temkin 55
becoming: as identity 27; path of 19; pursuit of 32; state of 26–28
beingness 29
Bel (the Assyrian) 44
belonging 20, 31, 33–35, 75–79, 96; and directing 3, 74–75, 78; idea of 32; and identity 1, 3–5; need for 70, 100; search for 11, 29, 61; sense of 2, 18, 21, 73–81, 97–99; struggle of 36; yearning for 52, 54
Benedetti, Robert 65

Index

Bhabha, Homi K. 34–37, 40
Binoche, Juliette 18
Bochner, Arthur 8
bogan 38
Bogan Hunters (television show) 39
Bogart, Anne 15, 74
Bolsheviks 56
Bourdieu, Pierre 17–18, 22, 90–92
Brazil 3
Brecht, Berthold 73
Brook, Peter 69
Brown, John Russell 14
Brown, Rena Cherry 16
Bruch, Debra 15
bullying 36, 81–82, 89

casting director 39; *see also* director (theatre); stereotypes
Catherine (blogger) 9
Caucasus, the 32
Cervonaro, Nicole 18, 21, 67–69, 74, 77
Chekhov, Anton 20
Cher 52
Chinoy, Helen-Krich 65
Christianity 36, 44–45
Cleary, Sam 76–77, 104
Clinton, Bill 48
Cohen, Robert 14, 80
Cole, A. L. 6, 10
Cole, Susan 65
Cole, Toby 65
Coleridge, Samuel Taylor 88–89
Conversations (play) 68
Cook, Amy 49
Copperwaite, Frederick 104
Core Mechanics 71
Cornell, Svante 57
Creswell, John 7, 9
cultural cringe 37–38
cultural difference 40, 74, 83–92, 97
cultural displacement 1–5, 8–10, 13; and directing 8, 73–74, 77, 79, 83–92; *see also* displacement
cultural identity *see* identity

Davis, Jodi 25–28, 30
defamiliarisation 83–92, 99
DeGraff, Geoffrey 27
Deleuze, Gilles 26–28
Denalli, James 104
Denzin, N. K. 8
Derrida, Jacques 90–92
diaspora (Armenian) 3, 32–34, 45, 50, 96
Diderot, Denis 30

difference 83–92, 99; as a cultural marker 36, 40; racial 89; shame regarding 59; theatre and 77, 97–99, 101; *see also* Bhabha, Homi K.; Bourdieu, Pierre; cultural difference; Derrida, Jacques
Dionysus 64
directing: deconstructing 64–73; field of 2, 6–7, 95; identity and 9, 29, 73–74, 99; as a journey 76–79, 81–82, 88, 92, 95; researching 10, 70–73; practice of 5, 8, 11, 29, 77, 81–92, 96; process 72, 76, 78; profession of 96–101; and theatre 15; *see also* belonging; cultural displacement; director's journey; identity; unhoming
director (film) 60, 66, 100
director (theatre): and identity 19–21, 27, 29, 91, 98; interviews with 11, 75–92; and marginalisation 39; profession of 40, 49, 71–72; role of 1–5, 10, 64–70, 73–74, 95–101; and self 73; status of 17–18; and theatre 88; *see also* theatre
director-producer 79
director-researcher 8, 54, 100
director's journey 79–82, 98–100, 103
disability 39
dislocation 2, 31, 76; of identity 34–35
displacement 1–5, 32–35, 37–38, 59, 81, 96
dissimulation 81–82
Dixon-Johnson, C. F. 45
Dog and Cat, The (play) 13, 100

Eden, Denise 104
Edwards, Gale 2, 102
Ego 24–25, 28
Egoyan, Atom 60
"eight ages of man" 29
Ellis, Carolyn 8
empathy 20, 49, 82, 88–89, 96
Erdoğan, Recap Tayyip 49
Erikson, Erik 24, 28–30, 74
Ethiopia 3
ethnicisms 37
ethnicity 36–37, 39, 45, 58, 74
European Court of Human Rights (ECHR) 3, 50
European Union 50

family 25, 80; and "home" 31; as social unit 30; theatre as 18–19, 21–22, 76–81, 98, 100
Fanon, Frantz 36
Fenech, Paul 39

field theory 17; *see also* Bourdieu, Pierre
Francis (Pope) 50
Freud, Sigmund 25, 28
Friedman, Susan 31, 33

Gallipoli 82, 91
genocide *see* Armenian Genocide
Georgia 56
Giannopoulos, Nick 39
Gibbs, Barney 104
Glover, Richard 39
Glover, Stephanie 79, 104
Golparian, Shaya 34–36
Gregory (monk) 46
Gregory the Illuminator 44
Gregory, William 65
Grotowski, Jerzy 19–20
Guattari, Félix 26

Hamid II (Sultan) 47
Haseman, Brad 6–7
Hayastan 44
Hayk 44
Hegel, Georg Wilhelm 27–29, 61
Herouni, Paris M. 44, 54
Herzig, Edmund 32
Hinton, Perry 85
Hitler, Adolf 48
Holland, François 48
Holman, David 82, 84–85
home: ancestral 3, 60; comforts of 13; concept/idea of 30–33, 77; and identity 32–33, 61; search for 60–61; sense of 4, 76; theatre as 78, 80; in Tsaghkadzor (example of) 58, *58*; and world 34; *see also* homing; unhomed; unhomely; unhoming
Home and Away (television show) 83
homeland 33, 61; Armenia as 45, 52, 54–55, 59; imaginary 53
homeless 35
homing 75–78; *see also* unhoming
hooks, bell 31, 34, 52
Housos (television show) 39
Hsiung, P. 9
Hudson, Chuck 104
hybridity, space of 40
Hytner, Nicholas 66

Id 25; *see also* Ego
identity 61, 100; and acting as a profession 70; actor's 30; Armenian 32–36, 38, 45, 58–60; becoming as 27; and belonging 1, 3–5; core 25, 28; cultural 21, 36, 56, 90; and directing 65, 76–77, 81–82, 91–92, 102; and Ego 28; ethnic 3, 8, 24–25, 33, 37, 45, 60, 96; external 25; formation of 28, 80, 95; group 24; and "home" 32–33, 61; individual 18–19, 25, 49, 80, 99; internal 25; loss of 29, 32, 95–96; negative 74; negotiating 36; and othering 38; seeking 24–40, 61, 74; and Self 4, 30; sense of 18, 22, 26, 35, 59, 73, 77, 80–82, 96–98, 103; struggle with 34, 75; *see also* Armenian-Australian identity; dislocation; Persian-Armenian-Australian; self-identity/self-identification
identity crisis 28–29, 74, 95
imperfection 37
in-between 20–21, 40, 96; and assimilation 35; space of 36–38; and other 33
Inwood, Michael 28
ipseity 5, 18, 22, 29–30
Iran 1–2, 13, 36–37
Islamic Revolution 2, 36
isolation 2, 79, 81–82, 102

James, William 6
John Paul II (Pope) 50
Jones, Michael 8

Kachoyan, John 65, 75, 104
Kaplan, Brett 33
Karabakh 51, 56–58, 60; *see also* Nagorno-Karabakh War
kata 71
Kelman, Dave 15
Kevorikian, Raymond 44
King, Charles 44
Kitchen Sink Collective 68–70
Knowles, J. G. 6, 10
Koca, Bogdan 2
Korwin-Kossakowski, Lucille 31
Kuiekn, Don 88
Kuritz, Paul 15
Kurkchiyan, Marina 32

Lachin corridor 57
Lamont, Leonie 38
Lane, Yoti 18–19
Lazare, Aaron 59
Lebanon 3, 39, 73
Lifted (play) 68
Lilley, Chris 39
Lincoln, Y. S. 8
Lippmann, Walter 85
longing 33; *see also* belonging

Lonnie, Ross 82, 84–86, 90–91
Louis XIV 14

Mamet, David 67–68, 72
Marinos, Lex 39–40, 66, 70–71, 73, 81, 104
Mashtots, Meshrob 46
McNamara, Carter 10
memory 31, 37, 50; constructed 52; *see also* schemas
memory work 48
Metcalf, Gabrielle 65, 67–69, 76, 104
Miall, David 88
Mignon, Jean-Pierre 71, 81, 104

Nagorno-Karabakh Autonomous Oblast (NKAO) 57
Nagorno-Karabakh Republic *see* Karabakh
Nagorno-Karabakh War 57
National Institute of Dramatic Arts (NIDA) 66
Neeme, Aarne 65, 69–71, 75, 91, 104
Neighbours (television show) 83
Nietzsche, Friedrich 60–61
Noah's Ark 45
Nonaka, Ikujio 8
No Worries (play) 82–87, *86*, 89, *90*, 92, 99

Oblast 57
other, the 2, 37–40, 52; and self 24; voice of 10
othered/othering 37–38, 55, 99
Ottoman Empire 46–50, 82

Pada, Roland 91
Pafumi, Helen 16
Parlakian, Nishan 45
Pashinyan, Nikol 51–52
Pattie, Susan 32–33
Payaslian, Simon 44
Persia/Persian 32, 46, 49
Persian-Armenian-Australian: cultural inheritance as 54; dialect 52, 60; identity as 4–5, 11, 21, 25, 32, 74, 100, 103
Phillips, Arthur Angell 37
Pickering, Michael 37–38
Pike, Shane 68–69
Pisters, Patricia 40
Polanyi, Michael 7–8
post-traumatic stress disorder (PTSD) 82, 89, 91
Practical Aesthetics 67
practice-led research 6–7
"Private Moment" 30

private/public spheres 35
psychosocial development 29
"Public Solitude" 30

racism 81–82, 92
Rafe, Jane 15
Ramachandran, Sujata 32
Reed-Danahay, D. 8
reflexivity 8–9
Return, concept of 33
Robertson, Geoffrey 49–50
Rogers, Matt 7
Rushdie, Salman 31, 35–36
Rutherford, Jonathan 40

Said, Edward 36, 40
Sargsyan, Serzh 51
Saroyan, William 44, 51
Schechner, Richard 30
schemas 55
Schön, Donald 7
Schuetz, Alfred 5
Schultz, Duane 28, 74
Schultz, Sydney 28, 74
Seidenstein, Ira 66, 69, 71, 81, 104
self 18, 27, 61; as a character 30; and directing 73–76, 78; Hegel's notion of 61; private/public 29–30; search for 4–5; searching for 24–40, 95; sense of 2–3, 11, 29, 78, 81, 99–101; situatedness of 8, 25; true/false 25; understanding of 26; *see also* ipseity
self-analysis 20
self-awareness 9, 15
self-exploration 1
self-identity/self-identification 11, 21, 24
self-mockery 37, 39–40
self-perception 36
self-protection 37
self-questioning 8–9
self-recognition 28
"selfsameness" 24, 27
Seljik Turks *see* Turks
Shakespeare, William 16
Shklovsky, Viktor 83–85, 87–88, 90, 92
simulacrum 91
Skuse, Anthony 75–77, 79–80, 104
Sökefeld, Martin 24, 27
Soviet Union 51, 53, 56–57, 59
Stanislavski, Constantin 19–20, 30, 73
state of becoming *see* becoming
stereotypes 37–39, 73, 83–92, 98; of/about Australia and Australians 1, 21, 39, 82, 84, 87, 99–100; breaking down 81

storytelling 90; by Armenians 45, 49; directors as 70, 73–74, 85, 96; realistic 20; and the theatre 15, 68, 95–96; traditions 14
Strasberg, Lee 30
Svirsky, Marcelo 27
Syria 3

tacit knowledge 7–8
Takeuchi, Hirotaka 8
Tan, Pearl 66, 91, 104
Ter Karapetyan-Chater, Hasmik 59
theatre: and the author (autoethnographic accounting by) 4–5, 13–14, 19–22, 26, 40, 71–74, 76, 95–101; director's role in 64–72, 77, 95–101; essence of 14–17; as social construct 17–19; *see also* director (theatre)
theatre director *see* director (theatre)
Theatre in Education (TIE) 82
theatrical storytelling *see* storytelling
third space 40
Tibet 54
Titizian, Maria 56
trace 9, 91
Trdat III (King) 44
Trumbull, Eric 66
Trump, Donald J. 49
Truscott, Steven 104

Tsaghkadzor 58, *58*
Tufankjian, Scout 3
Tumanyan, Hovhannes 13
Turkey 3, 46–51, 56, 58; and the United States 49
Turkmanchay Treaty 46
Turks 3, 45, 48–49; Seljik 46; Young 47

Uchitel, Joseph 66, 104
Uncle Jack (play) 81–92, *87–88*, 99
unhomed 35–36, 40, 75–76
unhomely 34–37, 52, 96
unhoming 32–35, 37–38; and directing 78, 98
United States 3, 49
Ussher, Clarence 44, 47

Velvet Revolution 51

Walton, Gregory 33
wog 37–38
World War I 47–48

Yashchin, Netta 70, 104
Yesterday's Hero (play) 68–69
Young Turks *see* Turks

Zandy, Janet 31, 77

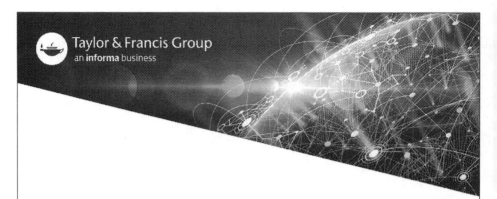

Taylor & Francis eBooks

www.taylorfrancis.com

A single destination for eBooks from Taylor & Francis with increased functionality and an improved user experience to meet the needs of our customers.

90,000+ eBooks of award-winning academic content in Humanities, Social Science, Science, Technology, Engineering, and Medical written by a global network of editors and authors.

TAYLOR & FRANCIS EBOOKS OFFERS:

- A streamlined experience for our library customers
- A single point of discovery for all of our eBook content
- Improved search and discovery of content at both book and chapter level

REQUEST A FREE TRIAL
support@taylorfrancis.com